50 More Tales of Flight

An Aviation Journey

OWEN ZUPP

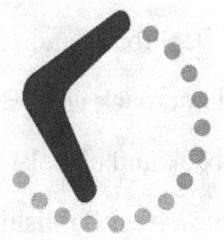

Copyright (c) Owen Zupp 2014

First published in 2014.

Registered Office P.O. Box 747, Bowral NSW 2576. Australia.

Author: Zupp, Owen 1964-

Title: 50 More Tales of Flight.

Owen Zupp

ISBN: 978-0-9874954-5-7 (Paperback)

ISBN: 978-0-9874954-4-0 (eBook)

Subjects: Aeroplanes. Piloting.-Biography. Air pilots.-Australia

All rights reserved. No part of this document may be reproduced, stored in a retrieval system, or transmitted in any form or by any means electronic, mechanical, photocopying, recording or otherwise without the permission of the copyright owner.

Also by Owen Zupp.

* 'Without Precedent' - (Hardcover, Paperback and eBook)

*'The Practical Pilot' (Paperback and eBook)

*'50 Tales of Flight. (Paperback and eBook)

*'Solo Flight'. (Paperback and eBook)

*'Down to Earth'. (Grub Street Publishing. 2007

www.owenzupp.com

***

Contents

IMAGES 4
THE AUTHOR 5
FOREWORD 6
1 THE JOURNEY BEGINS 1
2 WORK EXPERIENCE 7
3 AFTERMATH 13
4 THE NEXT STEP 19
5 THE NUN'S CAVE 29
6 THE ROAD LESS TRAVELLED 34
7 THE SIGNPOSTS OF THE SKY 40
8 LANDING GEAR DOWN.... OR IS IT? 44
9 ON THE RUN 52
10 CLOSE CALLS 58
11 A TRAGIC LOSS 66
12 WHEN THE DAY IS YOUNG 72
13 FLIGHT TO PARADISE 76
14 HALFWAY TO PARADISE 82
15 BEYOND PARADISE 88
16 JUST A COUNTRY AIRFIELD 94
17 A BALANCING ACT 98
18 A DIFFERENT APPROACH 105
19 SILENCE ALOFT 108
20 SO CLOSE...A WARTIME TRAGEDY 113
21 GHOSTS 120
22 A BOEING BAPTISM 124
23 TESTING TIMES 130
24 YOU, ME AND A TIGER MAKES THREE .. 136
25 FIRE IN THE SKY 142

Chapter	Title	Page
26	A WORLD CHANGED	148
27	A SACRED SITE	154
28	PEOPLE POWER	160
29	48 YEARS IN 3,000 FEET	164
30	FLYING WITH THE LORD OF THE RINGS	169
31	FLYING A GIANT	174
32	SEISMIC IN THE SKY	180
33	A CLASSIC FAREWELL	184
34	THE VIEW FROM ABOVE	190
35	HORNET'S NEST	194
36	BENEATH THE RADAR	204
37	IN THE HOVER	211
38	PEARL HARBOR	218
39	A GHOST IN THE MACHINE?	221
40	THE RIGHT MIX	224
41	SOMETHING DIFFERENT	229
42	WELCOME HOME	234
43	A FIGHTER'S WORLD	240
44	NO ESCAPE	244
45	CAPTURED IN TIME	248
46	A MATTER OF TRUST	254
47	FLY BY NIGHT	258
48	TOO OFTEN FORGOTTEN	262
49	CONTRAILS IN COMMON	266
50	MY LIFE OF FLIGHT	270
	ACKNOWLEDGEMENTS	274

For Mum.

(5th August 1923- 25th March 2014)

***

IMAGES

1. When the Day is Young. 33
2. Outback Delivery.. 33
3. Meeting the 'locals' in New Guinea... 65
4. A relic of New Guinea's wartime past. 65
5. A Japanese 'Zero' on Yap Island. 92
6. The poignant remains of the 'Hellcat' on Yap Island. 92
7. Frank Smith (seated in the Jeep) and his fellow Beaufort crew members. (Photo: E.Blight) 118
8. The Beaufort undergoing restoration in the 1990s. 118
9. The Tiger Moth... 146
10. Shining in the Sun. A Boeing 737. 146
11. Picture Perfect. Queenstown, New Zealand. 172
12. Seismic over Sydney. The Airbus A380 Formation. (Image:'Australian Aviation') 172
13. FA-18 Hornet Simulator. (Image:Tim Visser-'Blue Lens') 202
14. Another Seahawk takes to the Sky. 202
15. A Bell 'Kiowa' as seen through Night Vision Goggles. (NVG). 227
16. Something Different. The 'Cozy' peels away. (Image: 'Australian Aviation') 227
17. Captured in Time. The SNJ and its shadow become airborne on Oahu. 252
18. My daughter reflects on her grandfather's cockpit.................. 252

***

THE AUTHOR

Owen Zupp is an award-winning author and commercial pilot with 20,000 hours of flight time. He has flown all manner of machines from antique biplanes to globe-trotting Boeings and shared the journey with readers around the world in a variety of publications.

The son of a decorated fighter pilot, Owen was born into aviation. His flying career has taken him from outback Australia to the rugged mountain ranges of New Guinea, the idyllic islands of Micronesia and across the oceans of the world to the United States, Europe, Africa and beyond.

Whether witnessing rocket launches from 40,000 feet or circumnavigating Australia for charity in a tiny two-seat training aircraft, Owen has cherished every minute aloft. Flight is not merely his profession, it is his passion.

***

FOREWORD

As I have said many times before, flight is an amazing privilege and I am a very fortunate individual to fly.

The people and places that aviation has permitted me to encounter far exceeded anything that I could have imagined as a young boy. In those early years, I would sit on the airfield's edge for hours and watch the aircraft come and go.

Ultimately my own journey would take me around the world to amazing cities and almost hidden villages. I would fly the newest of jets off the production line and discover the remnants of aircraft in the deepest jungle. I would make new friends and bury old ones.

You, the reader, embraced my first '50 Tales of Flight' with an enthusiasm that truly humbled me. Now, here are '50 More Tales of Flight' that have been my privilege to experience and now my pleasure to share with you.

Thank you.

Owen Zupp

***

1

THE JOURNEY BEGINS

I'm not tall enough to see over the counter, but my eyes are wide with wonder. Everywhere people are bustling about and every wall is covered with huge glossy posters of aeroplanes. Some show the aircraft skimming through the clouds, while others are parked with picnickers beside them enjoying a day in the country. The clothes, haircuts and paint schemes are very 1970s.

Beside me stands my father, checking paperwork and signing forms, occasionally glancing down to check that his seven-year-old hasn't run away. I look up at him with impatient awe as he ensures that all is in order before we walk onto the flight line and take to the skies. Eventually he turns and moves towards the door and I follow like the shadow that I am. And then, there they are.

Tail after tail, wing after wing, all in a long neat row. Scarlet stripes and chequered bands brightly adorn the aeroplanes like a flying circus waiting to climb onto the invisible trapeze of the sky. My head is spinning as I endeavour to process the sights and sounds with a brain absolutely blurred with anticipation. I have flown with my father before, but today he has promised to let me fly the aeroplane. I am now tall enough to reach the wheel, so he believes that my time has come to learn the family trade.

Our machine is parked at the end of the line; a small two-seater Cessna 150. Its blue and white paint is shining and the letters "VH-EIS" are bold and black on its tail-fin. Dad opens the door and surveys the maintenance documents and lowers the wing flaps, explaining every step as he goes. I absorb bits and pieces but my heartbeat is drowning out his words. Outside, he walks around the aeroplane, waggling this and untying that. He samples the fuel from the tanks in the wings and checks the oil through a small access door on the engine cowling. He runs his hand along the smooth edge of the propeller and wipes the windscreen with a chamois. Finally it is my turn to climb aboard.

Dad moves the seat as high and as far forward as it will go and still he has to supplement my stature with a cushion. He asks me to turn the wheel left and right and move it fore and aft. He judges my performance and then clicks a seatbelt across my waist and pulls down a shoulder harness across my chest to attach near my hip. Once I am strapped in, he instructs me to release the belt and open the door; just in case I have to get out in a hurry. He seems satisfied with my performance, lashes me back in, slams the door and slips into the seat beside me.

The checklist is in his old fighter-pilot's head, and moments later Dad turns a key and the engine bursts into life. The propeller blades become a blur in front of me and the radios bark into life with strange voices screeching from the speaker over my head. Dad lifts a microphone from the dashboard and speaks in a similarly strange voice. Now there is a roar of the engine and we move forward with a roll and a bump over the grass and past the line of other Cessnas sitting wing-tip to wing-tip. We're on our way.

Onto the asphalt and past the open hangars, I am amazed at the aeroplanes that surround me: round engines, square engines, one engine or two engines. On the grass sits a mammoth with three massive tail fins, right beside a tiny biplane with an open cockpit. We taxi past a small tower and a fire truck before coming to a halt next to other stationary, but idling, aeroplanes.

Dad revisits the mental checklists and revs the engine up to a high power setting. The entire airframe buffets, straining against the brakes to be set free to fly. My father denies the request and turns a key which seems to deprive the engine of some of its power. He repeats the process and then starves it again by pulling a lever. Finally, he pulls yet another lever and the engine goes very quiet, chugging along with a low babble. Dad seems satisfied by all of these actions which he's described to me, and after yet more checks the time for takeoff has arrived.

At the runway's end he speaks through the microphone once more and the words, *"Cleared for takeoff!"* boom from the speaker. We pause for a moment and ahead of me lies the white zebra stripes of the runway's threshold and the "29R" painted equally boldly. A dashed line runs down the centre of the runway, disappearing into the distance. The engine returns to its fullest gusto and we begin to roll down the runway.

Faster, faster and faster still. The roar of the engine is complemented by the air rushing past my window and a rumbling coming up from the wheels, and then Dad eases the steering wheel back towards him and the nose rises from the ground. An instant later the two main wheels leave the ground and the rumbling and vibration from below disappears, and I realise that we are flying.

I look out the window to my side, as my favourite part of the takeoff is watching the world fall away. The fibreglass cover over the wheel still sits only a few feet from my door, but with every second that passes, the earth becomes ever more distant. The runway's tar is replaced by grass, then a river, then suburbia and shrinking red rooftops. I look ahead and beyond the aircraft's nose is the bluest of blue skies, and to my left Dad looks at me and smiles. I smile too.

As we leave the airport and city behind, the scenery ahead becomes rural. Green fields and farms dotted with sheds and livestock are barely discernible from our ever-increasing altitude. Dad lowers the nose of the aeroplane and reduces the power so that the little blue-and-white Cessna is now flying level. He motions for me to place my right hand on the steering wheel and shouts over the engine noise, "That's the control column, not a steering wheel." It's as if he can read my mind. He takes my left hand and sets it on a black-knobbed lever extending out from the instrument panel. "That's the throttle."

Dad moves the throttle and I observe the change in power on the dial and the engine noise in my ears. Then he rolls the control column to the left. Back to neutral and to the right and back to level flight. He pushes the control column forward and the nose lowers and I sense we're descending, he then pulls back and we are climbing once again. I have read all of these actions time and again and watched my father many times before, but now I am actually feeling it.

And then Dad takes his hands from the controls, holds them up in the air and says "Handing Over. You are flying." And yes, oh yes, I AM flying.

I wheel the Cessna about the sky as Dad sits back, arms folded but with his eyes hunting outside for other aircraft. He encourages me to be positive to the aeroplane, not to nudge it, but put it where I want it to be. Roll the wings left and right, push the nose up and down. Increase the power and reduce the power. In minutes, the thousands of words I have read are making far more sense and baking their way into my brain. Slowly, my concentration eases a little and I am able to take in my surroundings.

I wheel about the sky with a freedom and sense of control that I have never really felt before. I am only a boy, but this seems to be the most natural feeling in the world to me. I have no sense of fear at all, no trepidation. Only the deepest sense of joy. My eyes struggle to keep up with my racing mind as I digest the beauty of the world below and the vast expanse of the blue that surrounds me. Amidst a sea of thoughts I am actually putting the aeroplane where I want it without thinking about. I'm flying! I'm flying! I want to scream it out to the world.

Dad looks at his watch and points back towards the airport. I follow his command and now the pastures give way to the approaching suburbs and we descend from our vantage point above the world. Dad calls "taking over" but encourages me to rest my hands on the controls and follow his inputs as he brings the Cessna back towards the runway. The three black strips with their zebra markings and dotted lines loom ahead. Dad points to another aircraft just to our right who seems stationary in space as he parallels our path through the sky.

Between radio calls and the flaps extending from the wing beside me, Dad explains what he is doing at every step. He interrupts himself momentarily and motions to a bird approaching ahead of us. He eases the Cessna slightly to the left and the bird passes by my wing tip. For an instant I could swear that he was staring at me with the same intent that my eyes were set on him. I smiled, he didn't. I was a stranger in his realm.

He slipped away as quickly as he had approached and now I watched the airport grow ever closer and feel my father's subtle inputs through the pressure on my own hands. As the stripes disappeared beneath the aeroplane's nose, Dad eases back on the throttle and control column as the final few feet of altitude disappear and our main wheels begin to roll along the runway. Only then do I feel my Dad relax the back pressure on the control column and allow the wheel beneath the nose to fly equally smoothly onto the ground.

Our land-locked journey to the runway's end was relived in reverse as we made our way back to our parking spot. Dad brought the Cessna to a halt and completed yet more checks before he drew out the red-handled lever to starve the engine of fuel and bring silence to our ears once again. Click, click, click; the last switches were flicked off and the keys placed upon the dashboard. The aeroplane was now safe but lifeless and my flight had come to an end.

Dad smiled at me again and asked, "How was that?" For once his chatty shadow was lost for words and I struggled to find an answer. It is an answer that I still struggle to frame in a sentence more than four decades later.

For although it wasn't my first flight on that sunny May morning, it was the first day that I really flew. It was the first time that I truly felt absolute freedom in the three dimensions. I had watched the world tilt outside my window and looked down upon a bird in flight. The fuse was lit and my boyhood interest had exploded into a burning passion. On that day I realised that my dream of flight was so much more than a fanciful sense of wonder pencilled into my schoolboy drawings.

Flight was real, it was tangible. Whereas before I gazed upon aeroplanes as they passed overhead, I would henceforth always imagine myself in the cockpit looking down. One way or the other, I was determined that it was to become my world, my realm, my three dimensions. On that day, more than any other, my journey had begun.

***

2

WORK EXPERIENCE

I've hardly slept a wink. This night the ticking of the clock was frustrating rather than hypnotic as I waited for the hour to arrive. Now I hear the familiar sounds of my father stirring: running taps, flicking light switches and the jangle of his uniform shirt as wings, pens and identity cards bounce off one another. Today I'm going to work with Dad.

The airport is dark and deserted at 4am, except for the glow of light from a row of windows atop a low brick building. Inside the world is alive with pilots at work, compiling flight plans on sloping glass benches surrounded by walls covered with charts. Slide rules and carbon paper are flicking at high speed as the air routes are translated into times and distances and submitted to the waiting gentlemen behind the counter.

Dad chats with the meteorological officer before settling down to his own flight plan. After years of plying the same airspace, the numbers flow from his head and onto the paper at an impressive rate. He checks them against the charts, double-checks his mathematics and then slides the plan across the counter for approval and the *clunk* of the Briefing Officer's time stamp. I have a bare Student Pilot's Licence, but this is a whole other world. Soon we are on our way again, but first there is one pit stop to make.

Next door, the briefing office is also filled with pilots, but here they are drinking cups of coffee and biting into slices of warm toast. My Dad contravenes standard family regulations and buys me a flavoured milkshake and a donut....at 4:30am! I can't believe my luck and marvel at the real freedom of flight as I take the first sip.

I am still juggling my breakfast as we cross the hangar floor to the awaiting Beechcraft Queen Air. The white twin-engined aircraft is emblazoned with stripes of black and red and the crest of the NSW Ambulance Service and sparkles under the bright lights dangling from the hangar's roof. The Flight Nurse welcomes me aboard as she goes about her equipment checks and Dad goes about his own routine of checking paperwork and log books.

Today is a routine transfer for the Air Ambulance, but the pace at which the day is unfolding makes my head spin. In the cockpit Dad adjusts my seat and harness and scans the instrument panel before descending down the stairs and beginning his daily inspection of the aeroplane. Flaps, landing gear, fuel and oil. Around the airframe he walks, pausing, pushing and pulling. As Dad completes his lap of the Queen Air, the nurse gives her own "thumbs up" to indicate her readiness. We all climb aboard and Dad heaves the door closed and lowers the handle firmly, locking it in place. He gives it another shove, just to check that it is indeed locked before turning on his heel and climbing into the cockpit.

I sit there silently. Having flown with my father so many times, I know to speak only when spoken to in the aeroplane. As the "tug" drags us from the hangar Dad scrolls over the rotary checklist on the instrument panel until he reaches the checklist titled "Before Start". Now we wait for the tug to stop and disconnect the tow bar as I stare out the side window where, every few seconds, our red rotating beacons are light up the darkness. Inside the cockpit, there is just the faint glow of the dials illuminating my Dad's face as he now waits for the cue to start.

The engineer raises his hand with one finger extended to the sky. "Starting One", Dad calls through the small open window beside him as he turns the magneto switch with his left hand and juggles a lever in his right. The combination sends the propeller whirring and then the engine roaring and the Queen Air comes to life, breaking the pre-dawn silence. The airframe shudders as he brings the second engine on line and my excitement level kicks up another notch.

More checklists and "thumbs up" and then Dad's voice comes through the headsets pressed tight over my ears. I let him know that I can hear him "loud and clear" before he turns away and transmits his requests to the waiting control tower. With approval granted, he eases up the throttles and we move smoothly away from the hangar; then he touches the brakes to check they are functioning. The long line of green lights ahead mark the taxiway and he hands over to me to taxi the Queen Air as straight as I can along the dark strip of asphalt.

To me, the bumping of the nosewheel as it strikes every green light indicates that I am travelling well, but the grimace on my Dad's face indicates that the bumping doesn't offer the smoothest of rides for the nurse and any potential passengers. My first lesson learned, I nudge ever so slightly to one side. All the while the chatter over the radio increases and tells me that the airport is waking up, as the airliners about me shake off the night and ready for the day ahead.

Near the runway's end, Dad tells me to bring the aircraft to a halt. There are more checks and engine runs to complete and a last word with the nurse in the cabin before he finally tells the tower that we are ready to go. The single row of green taxiway lights now give way to a massive array as we line up on the threshold. The points of light extend far into the distance as Dad opens the throttles and sets the Queen Air on its way.

The terminals and stirring airliners rush by outside as the rumbling of the wheels on tar grows louder. I watch my father's eyes hunting inside and out of the cockpit as he eases the nose into the sky and the rumbling wheels thump into their stowage and go silent. We are flying.

Dad is deep in concentration as my eyes drift outside to watch the lit coastline fall away below. I think of all of the people who are just waking while I have already seen so much of the day. Our lights blink into the darkness and the whirring of the electric motors tells me that the flaps are retracting to their home in the wings. The engine's roar diminishes to a slightly more subtle hum under Dad's hand as we turn to set course beyond the mountains.

The first hint of sun is lighting the cloud-tops ahead, but the land below remains shrouded in darkness. As we climb into the sky I feel as if we are drawing the line between night and day rather than experiencing the rotation of the earth. Soon the glow of the dials has given way to the glare of the dawn and the black blanket turns to a landscape of long shadows.

I look towards Dad and want to speak, but hesitate. He is not deep in concentration speaking on the radio; rather, he is looking at the world below with a half-smile on his face. It is a look of contentment that I see every time he flies and it inspires me even more to one day share his sky in my own right. He senses my gaze and looks towards me, still smiling. "See the heading?" he asks. "See the airspeed?" I do. "You're cleared to 8,000 feet...handing over."

I grasp the substantial control column of the Queen Air. It is white in colour with patches worn back to the metal through years of use. Buttons that activate radios and disconnect autopilots protrude from the yoke, so I decide to keep my fingers to myself and fly this magic carpet. To my left and right, tall puffy clouds are growing with the day and whizz by my wingtips at a speed too great to fathom. They offer a slight bump and a sense of speed that the smooth clear air cannot convey.

A long level layer of cloud looms ahead between me and my goal of 8,000 feet. Dad has frequently had me flying on instruments so I set my scan to the significant dials on the panel ahead of me. Wings level...nose attitude....constant heading....airspeed...and back again. Wings level...

We close in on the cloud in a matter of seconds but the impact with the droplets of vapour is silent. Only the rush of the air and the engines is to be heard as the grey blanket envelopes us. I am concentrating intensely, forcing my eyes from dial to dial. As I do, the cloud starts to become lighter and brighter until it gives way to the brilliant blue of the morning sky. I raise my eyes the cloud layer whistles by and the Queen Air's shadow skips along its milky surface like a high-speed travel companion. My excitement is incomparable.

As we reach 8,000 feet I lower the aircraft's nose and Dad cues me to retard the throttles, trim the aircraft and set the "mixtures". Finally, after more checks and actions, the Air Ambulance is settled in the cruise and on its way to its destination. Dad offers me the autopilot, but I kindly decline and I can see that it's an answer he appreciates. I want to make the most of every moment and feel the aeroplane beneath my hands, for one day I want this to be my office.

I look at my father once again and ponder at his relaxed state. It is a face that I rarely see at sea level where ringing phones and heavy traffic frustrate him to his wit's end. Here he is totally at ease. His eyes wander about the cockpit in a cursory confirmation that all is well as he logs another time and changes another frequency. It all seems to be second nature to him and I marvel at that fact.

Through the curtains the nurse emerges with a warm smile and a hot cup of tea for Dad. Outside the beauty of the countryside is laid out in a magnificent panorama that changes by the minute. I cannot imagine a better way to greet each day and spend my life. I am determined. One day the sky will be my office too. One day.

***

3
AFTERMATH

Many years ago I earned my keep as a paramedic. More to the point, my salary routinely made its way directly into the bank account of the Royal Aero Club as I paid for each and every cherished hour of flying training. Often I would arrive at the aero club well before the flight and then loiter a little more once I had landed. I enjoyed the surroundings of planes and pilots and the constant hum of chatter about all things flying.

One such sunny morning I was standing by the counter, chatting with the instructors and looking out through the glass entrance of the clubhouse. One after the other, aircraft leapt into the sky to make the most of the clear blue overhead. The booking sheets were full as instructors scurried past me, hurrying between lessons. And then it all seemed to come to a screeching halt.

The unmistakable wail of the "crash horn" pierced the air and aeroplanes and people froze where they stood. Looking out over the airport it now resembled a motionless diorama with the exception of a growing plume of smoke. Just beyond the tree line at the airport's edge, an unmistakeable thick, black, billowing cloud rose into the air. An aircraft had crashed.

For a moment I was frozen to the spot, then the paramedic instinct kicked in and I began to walk towards the door. I was virtually at the crash site and I knew that I had to respond. One of the instructors, Jeremy, offered to lend a hand and followed me to my car where I threw on my white overalls with crests on the shoulders and "Ambulance" boldly embroidered in red across the back.

I drove at a measured pace around the airport perimeter with one eye on the traffic and the other on the black plume that still climbed skyward. Within minutes I was standing beside the flashing blue lights of a lone police car and a pale young constable calling for assistance on his radio. He looked at me and said simply, "They're all dead", as he pointed towards the factory roof from which the smoke was now trickling.

Grabbing my first-aid kit, I left Jeremy with the constable and walked briskly down the driveway towards the factory. The huge sliding door was wide open, but a wall of smoke made me feel most unwelcome. I lowered my kit to the ground and moved closer, guided on by a broad ray of sunlight that penetrated the gloom. I cautiously entered the building, wary of becoming overcome by the acrid smoke. Gradually my eyes adjusted and I could see that the light was pouring in through a jagged hole in the roof and from the edge of which seemed to hang an aeroplane.

Tangled amongst framework and sheet metal, the aircraft sat with its nose down as if frozen an instant before impacting the factory floor. However, it had already impacted the roof with a violent force. The roof groaned under the load and small pockets of flame were about me as I edged towards the wreckage. And there they sat. Still in their seats, restrained by their harnesses, but blackened and lifeless. Frozen in the instant of impact. Passengers who only minutes before had undoubtedly been caught up in excited conversation before the horror arrived. I checked for any sign of life, but there was none. Amidst the trauma I noted the unblemished skin of one chap beneath a woollen jumper and strangely noted how this natural fabric provided such sound protection against the heat. There was nothing that I could do.

I stepped back and paused for a moment. My eyes were watering and my breathing a little laboured. Then a human groan invaded my transfixed state and I was drawn back to the present, looking around in the darkness for any sign of life. I moved away from the aircraft and towards the sound. Now I heard a banging on the roof overhead. Were there survivors?

He was lying on the floor, his clothes and hair burnt from his peeling body. Gasping for breath and unable to form words his pain transcended speech. One leg lay at an awkward angle and his helplessness reached deep into my guts. About him were footprints tinged with blood. Had someone been here before me?

My training was to leave this poor soul unmoved and seek assistance; but I couldn't leave him. The roof overhead continued to creak and bang and I wondered if it was on the verge of collapse, so I resolved to drag him clear as best I could. I half lifted him with my arms beneath his armpits and pulled him towards the open door and clear air. His pain must have been beyond compare and guilt overwhelmed me that I may be hurting him even more, but I wanted him away from the immediate danger of fire and falling framework. Laying him there in the sunlight his breathing seemed a little easier; but only a little. His airway was obviously scorched and swelling and soon there would not be a clear path for oxygen to reach his lungs.

Looking up I saw the welcome forms of my fellow paramedics advancing towards me and I became aware of the increasing presence of howling sirens and barking two-way communications. Uniformed bodies were growing in numbers as I handed my patient over to my mates with a thumbnail sketch of what I knew about his state.

Hanging onto faint hope, I re-entered the factory. Perhaps those footprints meant someone else had survived? The air was clearing and now I could make out the aircraft at a distance, but still no other human forms except those still securely fastened in their seats. Still the roof creaked and groaned, but the banging had increased...and was that a voice? I was certain it was. I looked around for a stairwell, but couldn't readily see how I could get onto the roof. Again I felt helpless.

Now uniforms with equipment began to filter into the factory behind me. I pointed towards the roof and relayed my hope of another survivor. I was almost knocked over in the rush as the rescue crews set about gaining access above. I was rapidly disappearing into the formal, concerted effort of the combined emergency services. Hoses were unravelling and manpower was to be found in every direction. I moved back to where I had left my patient and found him being treated and readied for transport. I could not see any response from his eyes like I had seen before as we wrapped him in sheets of silver foil and lifted him onto a stretcher.

The activity around us became frenzied as they had found another person alive on the roof. Emergency service workers darted by, as did a TV cameraman with his hefty rig on his shoulder. I wondered how he had gained access and what good he could possibly achieve.

Meanwhile, I took up one end of the stretcher while a third paramedic held high the bottle feeding the intravenous line. We moved back down the driveway towards where I had parked my car and a waiting helicopter. Across the street and up the gutter, we had to travel cross-country over a vacant lot and I felt every bump and tuft of grass as the stretcher heaved until we lifted its wheels clear of the ground. Just when the journey was nearly complete, a media helicopter swept low overhead, kicking up dirt and threatening to blow the silver foil blanket from our patient and contaminate his wounds. A small female paramedic threw herself over the stretcher as a shield as I swore at the thoughtless vultures.

Soon the rescue helicopter's rotors began to turn and coat me in dust. Within minutes the unmistakable thumping grew quiet and the chopper disappeared into the distance. Now I just stood there with nothing to do. The on-duty crews had the situation under control and the survivor from the roof was now treated and transported. All that remained was emergency vehicles parked on odd angles with open doors and officers attending to the routine tasks that follow a critical incident. The scene was like a sports stadium after the last of the crowd has left and the once vital arena falls dormant. Jeremy had long since left, so I gathered up my gear and walked to my car, looking down at my soot-stained overalls and my skinned knuckles. I surveyed my hands, but had no idea when that had happened. I took a breath, started my car and drove off.

That night the news channels broadcast footage of the scene and confirmed that there was another passenger on the roof who was now in a "stable" condition. Personal details of my patient were released but I didn't want to hear them. I could still see his agony and feel it at my core. Ultimately, with burns to 90 per cent of his body, he lost his battle within hours. The next day his photograph was on the front page, a young, smiling, vital face. I can still see his other face today.

While scenes of death are commonplace in the life of a paramedic, the loss of an aircraft, pilot and passengers doubly impacted me. I was training to be a pilot and despite every lesson I had absorbed in the classroom to that time, the twisted airframe and charred bodies I had seen spoke volumes more. They spoke of the potentially unforgiving nature of flight and that tragedy can be only moments away. The airspeed indicator projects the numbers we fly by, but when man and machine meet the earth, out of control and at speed, the outcome is horrendous.

The sights, smells and sounds of that day have never left me. The loss of that aircraft and the souls on board has stayed with me so vividly for so many years. For me, it is not about sirens and police tape, helicopters and fire-hoses. For me, my memory is the aftermath.

***

4

THE NEXT STEP

There was no escaping it. After six weeks of waiting the day had arrived, or, more accurately, it had emerged from a sleepless night. It was still dark as I drove into the airport with my father and only a few offices emitted a glow from the windows in their back rooms. In contrast, the flight briefing office near the runway's edge was a hive of activity, with bright fluorescent lights and charter pilots checking weather forecasts before submitting flight plans. If today went well, perhaps I would one day be checking charts and drinking coffee before the sun had peeped its head above the horizon. Only today would tell. Today I would give my utmost to become a licensed commercial pilot.

My father had been my flight instructor, but that morning he kicked me out of the car like a duckling is kicked out of the nest. His military training was black and white and there was no room for soft edges. I was ready, so just go and do it like you've done it before, was his philosophy. Nerves and trepidation didn't enter into the argument, just do what you were trained to do, son.

So there I stood at the glass-topped, inclined bench in the briefing office. The rain pitter-pattered outside and my heart thumped in my chest. The weather forecasts were not promising, but that was no surprise as I had gotten wet just walking from the car. It was still a couple of hours until the "examiner of airmen" would start his day, but I was intent on having every piece of information at my fingertips before he arrived. Still, as I pored over the charts and weather printouts, I struggled to find any route that was suitable for the rules of visual flight that would govern my flight test. I had to be able to see where I was going and navigate by looking out the window. Flying solely by reference to instruments was still a way down the road for me.

These were the days when all licence test were conducted by examiners from the Department of Aviation; not delegates. As such, if the weather intervened, it would be another six weeks before another booking would be available, so I was desperate to fly if it was at all possible. Fortunately, the examiner explained he felt the same way, as I shook his hand. John was a former Air Force transport pilot with close-cropped black hair just beginning to grey in his sideburns. He reviewed the weather forecasts and agreed with my bleak outlook, however he also offered that he was at the airport all day should the weather improve. In addition, he took me to his office and conducted the mandatory pre-flight examination of questions relating to my aircraft and the rules and regulations. All those boxes were ticked, so now all I had to do was fly!

For the next four hours I pestered the meteorologist at the briefing office for any glimpse of a positive trend. The grey skies had lifted somewhat at the airport, but I needed clear air farther afield to complete the flight test. Around lunchtime, there was a glimmer of hope. The weather to the north was clearing and if I departed in an hour, I might just be able to manage to time it correctly. I phoned my father, who promptly responded by appearing at the briefing office and dragging me off to eat something. It was a wise move.

With a full stomach, and armed with my forecasts, I entered John's office with my summation. He flipped through the pages with a doubtful look before lowering the paper to the table and asking how soon I could be ready. After I answered that I had been ready for hours, he scribbled a route down on a pad and passed it to me with an instruction to submit a flight plan and meet him with the aircraft outside the briefing office in an hour.

I walked quickly back and submitted my flight plan to the briefing officer after a final chat with the "Met Man". Both seemed sceptical at my endeavour, but wished me luck nonetheless before bringing down the big red stamp to approve my flight plan. It was "game on" and my excitement was now smothering any lurking doubts.

The aircraft sat on the ramp waiting. Marked VH-HAB, the Piper Arrow IV was a single-engined aeroplane with four seats and retractable landing gear. It was a light, dirty-brown colour with mustard, red and black pinstripes and a matching flash on the tail. Inside it was well equipped and "boasted" high-backed seats covered in brown velour. It was not my preference for a paint scheme or decor, but this aeroplane was set to be my best friend for the next few hours.

When John arrived at the aircraft I treated him like a commercial passenger as the rules of the flight test dictate. I had to brief him on safety equipment, emergency exits, what not to touch, what bits were dangerous, when not to speak and on and on. With nothing left to say, we both strapped into the Piper Arrow and John assumed the mantle of the silent examiner as I went about my checklists.

Thankfully, the aircraft started and I logged the time and fuel status before moving off towards the runway. As I completed the last of my procedures, the weather was becoming clearer by the minute and my hopes lifted. I checked the door and John's seat belt one last time as hanging a belt out the door was an old examiner's favourite trick. All was in order and we were cleared for takeoff.

As the nose lifted into the sky, I touched the brakes to stop the wheels spinning before retracting them into the wells within the wings. The dull thump and the extinguished light confirmed that the wheels were up and I rolled into a turn to the right, setting course to the north.

The "escape route" was via an aerial transit lane that kept light aircraft clear of the traffic from the nearby major airport. It involved steering via a series of substantial ground features, flashing strobes and brightly painted water tanks rather than religiously steering by the compass. To keep beneath the airliners the initial cruising altitude was also minimal, so I scooted from feature to feature, ticking them off on my map. Just as I was about to exit the far end of my aerial channel, a gleaming white airliner passed overhead, capturing both of our attention. Its gleaming white body was finished with a vast scarlet tail featuring a flying kangaroo. It seemed to swoop effortlessly above us, lining up for its final approach to land. Stunning sights like these were one of the reasons that I yearned to fly.

Free of the city limits and the confines of its airspace, I crossed a deep green waterway and an old iron bridge, both of which signalled that it was time to climb higher. A few friendly white clouds still lingered, but nothing to prevent the Arrow taking me to a greater height where I could also gain a better lay of the land. Heavily wooded paddocks and rising ranges passed beneath me with only the occasional road offering any indication as to my location. I persisted with steering my planned heading on the compass and checking my watch as I awaited my next flight-planned turning point. Fortunately, right on time, a little hamlet came and went slightly down the right-hand side of the aircraft. I recalculated, adjusted the heading to steer, checked my fuel and continued on my way. John nodded silently but positively from the right-hand seat.

For the first time I began to feel comfortable. Not confident, but comfortable. After such a delayed and anxious start, I was now where I loved to be. Looking beyond my wingtips I could see the coastline to one side and rugged bushland to the other. All the while the earth slipped beneath me at two-and-a-half-miles every minute over terrain that explorers and pioneers had slaved to conquer. I felt like the most fortunate person on earth.

The magical moments continued to tick over and I counted them down on the flight plan perched on my knee. Our first landing point lay ahead but I still could not see it. I could see the village beside me, the massive power lines and even the large drive-in screen right beside the airport, but not the runway itself. I continued to make my radio calls in hope of sighting the airfield, but my comfortable feeling was shrinking as I shifted in my seat. John obviously sensed my concern, but I dared not look his way. Instead I scanned the horizon for anything resembling an airport. A windsock, anything, *please!*

Then, there it was. Two thin black strips of asphalt crossing each other. Thank heavens!

John asked me to fly a few takeoffs and landings before we came to a stop. Some landings were totally regulation, while some were without the flaps and others were with all the flaps to stop in the shortest possible distance. Another was without engine power and, on one occasion, John told me to abort the landing at the last minute and return to the sky. Finally we agreed to bring the Arrow to a halt and stop for some refreshments in the Aero Club.

As we drank our soft drinks, John was cordial but maintained the necessary distance of one sitting in judgement of the other. I spoke with him about his Air Force days and he told me that he had flown the deHavilland Caribou and recalled its stunning ability to land just about anywhere, no matter how short or how rough. I could've sat there all day and listened to his recollections but there was a flight test to complete and the end of daylight was a consideration.

I checked our aeroplane over one more time, confirmed our fuel quantities and completed a few written tables for John. With us both satisfied, we climbed aboard and set course once again. The Arrow clipped along and the weather had now cleared altogether allowing me to see beyond the beautiful mountain range. But now John told me to descend to 500 feet and find my way without the benefit of the view.

My father had been rigorous with my low-flying training, so I relished this opportunity. I descended to a safe height and readied to fly the aircraft with a bare minimum of time looking at the chart. Fortunately, a railway-line led from my current position to where John wanted me to be, so I simply set the tracks in the windscreen and followed the line. This seemed relatively straightforward, still I sensed John was smirking and very quickly I realised why. The railway line disappeared.

In fact, it had entered a tunnel, leaving me to climb away from the hilltop ahead of me, wondering where my train-tracks had gone. Fortunately, by the time I had caught my breath, I spotted the railway emerging from the other side of the hill and I'm pretty sure I heard John laugh at that point. Either way, he seemed in a good mood and instructed me to amend my flight plan to take us both home via the quickest route.

I climbed back up to a safer height, got my bearings and drew a line on my map. I made the necessary calculations, checked the latest weather and readied to broadcast my intentions on the radio when I sensed something wasn't adding up. An immediate left turn would see me heading home, but I held steady for a minute or two. As I double-checked, I noticed John rubbing his chin and looking out the window. What the hell was it? Then the penny dropped.

John had flown Caribous, and in fact he had flown them in the airspace out to my left between where we were and home. And that was restricted military airspace! I confirmed my suspicions and then set about drawing a whole new set of lines and working out a new series of calculations that would see me skirt around the Air Force's no-go zone. I had gone within 30 seconds of failing my commercial licence test, but the near-miss seemed to release the tension in the cockpit and John became more than cordial, he became genuinely friendly.

As we flew around the perimeter of his old airspace he even pointed out a couple of features and related a few more tales. Some examiners were known to become chatty to distract the candidate, but John seemed relaxed and enthused. Nevertheless, I continued to fly as well as I possibly could as I knew that I still had nearly an hour to go before the flight test would draw to a close.

As we rounded the final corner of the restricted airspace and set course for home, John placed the "hood" on my head. The hood is a lightweight device that resembles an oversized peak on a cap, extending six inches forward and curving down on both sides. Its purpose is to restrict the pilot's vision, thereby depriving them of a horizon for reference. With the hood in place, John had me fly the aircraft solely by reading my instruments as if I was in cloud. My licence would not allow me to fly in this way, but the examiner needed to see that I could keep the aeroplane the right way up if I inadvertently entered cloud. For 15 minutes I turned, climbed and descended upon his command.

When he removed the hood I was over the dramatic drops of the mountain ranges with its carved waterways and spectacular cliff faces. It was stunning and was made even more so by the setting sun behind me. The lengthening shadows concealed small valleys and stretched peaks for miles. Ahead lay the lower lands of the basin and the short run home. I was very weary but I was nearly there.

With 10 miles to go, I completed my final checks and ensured that

John was safe and strapped in. As I reached for the radio to change the channel, the engine noise fell away and the aircraft's nose pitched down. The engine had failed.

A split-second after my heart had skipped a beat; I looked down to see John's hand on the throttle. He had pulled the lever back to simulate an engine failure and now I had to deal with it. I immediately went into my initial actions and set the once-powerful aeroplane to glide back to earth. I looked for a field to land in and sighted a small airport not too far away, but could I make it? I looked at my altitude again. Yes, I could get there.

I advised John of my intention to glide to the airport to our right and continued to simulate the actions of attempting to restart the engine, brief the passenger and broadcast a "Mayday call". In this case I used the radio to warn any traffic at the airport that I was gliding towards the field and arriving in a less than conventional manner. All the while, John sat there leaning on one elbow, emotionless. And all the while, I was sweating.

My heart began to rise in my chest as it became increasingly apparent that this was going to have a good outcome. When I was assured of reaching the runway, I lowered the landing gear and then some flaps and then all of the flaps. We crossed the fence at the right speed and height before touching down right on the money. I was ecstatic and John seemed equally pleased as he told me to "Take us home".

This final instruction I completed with pleasure, and for the first time I now suspected that I had passed the test. After our arrival I parked the aircraft and shut it down, being very careful not to make a stupid mistake at the last hurdle. After the propeller had come to a halt and the last checklist had been read, John reached across to me, smiled and shook my hand. It was one of the greatest moments of my life.

As he climbed out and made his way to his office, I sat there and savoured the moment. I was absolutely exhausted but with a sense of achievement that schoolwork had never really provided me. It was growing darker by the minute and I realised that it was well beyond the end of John's normal working day. I gathered my things and headed briskly towards the Department of Aviation offices to complete the paperwork.

As I walked along the road, my father stepped out from behind a car. "No good?" he questioned. "No. I passed!" He had seen John return without me and then, eventually, my seemingly forlorn figure came into view. He had misread the signals but then shook my hand with more vigour than I had ever felt. He seemed as elated as me, although a firm handshake was as expressive as he generally became.

John duly signed the paperwork and stamped it to certify that I was now a commercial pilot. He congratulated me again and I still couldn't believe that it was true. He assured me that it was.

That day was a major step in a career that I enjoyed beyond compare. In so many ways, that three-hour flight cracked the door on what an aviation career is all about. There were magical moments and breathtaking scenery, times of fatigue, fright and elation. Expect the unexpected and never rush into a response. Even at the end of the day, when you're tired and home lies ahead in the window, remain vigilant. The flight is never over until the aircraft is lashed down or parked in the hangar.

Aviation is a career under the microscope. Like that flight test, a pilot will continually be under scrutiny and expected to demonstrate a level of proficiency on a regular basis. Studying, simulators and check flights are just a part of a pilot's life. They are not necessarily the most enjoyable aspect of a flying career, but they are as certain as the sunrise. The same magical sunrise that all pilots are privileged to witness from the best seat in the house.

***

5

THE NUN'S CAVE

By all accounts, it was just another charter flight. A lone doctor, flown to a remote community to provide medical checks and medications. Nothing out of the ordinary and, for me, the inevitable sitting around and waiting that charter pilots know so well. However, from the time that the runway at Balgo Hill loomed ahead, it started to become apparent that this was no ordinary day.

While the rich, red dirt runway was nothing new, off the far end the sky was filled with what seemed to be thousands of soaring hawks. They seemed to be disappearing into the very ground beyond the airport and emerging just as mysteriously. At that stage my only concern was their presence if I aborted the landing and climbed towards them. This never eventuated, and I parked my twin-engined Cessna beneath the clearest blue Kimberley sky.

The doctor waved goodbye through the open window of the dust-covered four-wheel drive, mumbling something about when he might be back; give or take an hour. I put the silver foil sunscreens in place inside the Cessna's cabin, dressed the seatbelts and set up the cockpit for departure...whenever that may be.

Still curious about the swirling birds I began to wander along the airfield's edge towards the distant perimeter. As I drew closer, the amazing scene ahead of me became apparent. For the ground seemed to fall away dramatically and the hawks were actually flying into openings on the side of a cliff face. Balgo sat atop a Mesa-like structure, except this sheer drop extended for as far as the eye could see. It was not so much a canyon as the remnants of a massive inland body of water, now drained.

As I peered over the edge, fascinated by the hawks, I could see more holes in the rock-face where the birds rested, but where water probably lapped in millions of years ago. It was mid-afternoon and if I squinted tightly and let my mind drift I could imagine this enormous inland lake filled with prehistoric water as Diprotodons wandered around behind me.

My time machine was interrupted by the voice of another who was obviously intrigued by my pensive state. A tribal elder, his face bore deep creases and his eyes were rich with character. We chatted quite some time and then he guided me further around the edge and beyond the main group of birds. We came upon a very small hole just in from the cliff face with an old wooden ladder poking out. The hole was barely wide enough for a grown man's shoulders, but my new friend gestured towards the ladder. He then uttered simply, "The Nun's Cave".

With the optimism of youth and the build to match, I threw down my backpack before slipping down the ladder, beyond the surface and into an amazing cave. It had seemingly been formed by the inland ocean washing in and eroding the rock face and perhaps the opening that I scampered down had once been a blowhole. But now it was a cave, opening towards the west and the lowering sun, offering an unsurpassed view of the extensive gorge.

Inside the cave it was cool, sheltered from the Kimberley sun. In various corners were low stone platforms like shelves and on some rested the remnants of burned-down candles. My guide informed me that, many years ago, nuns from the mission would come to this cave and seek solace or hold small services. And even though this cave was his ancestors' spiritual land long before Europeans set foot in Australia, my new friend respected this as "sacred ground".

I explored further within the cave and, aside from candles, there were rosaries, small crosses and even an old bible. Its pages were a little wrinkled, but considering the passage of the years, it was in remarkable condition. The dry central Australian air had preserved the entire scene as it had been left, decades before. It was a time capsule.

My friend ascended the ladder, assuring me that he would fetch me when the doctor had completed the clinic. So now I stood there, alone in this hallowed hall of nature's making. I retrieved the small backpack that I had thrown down the hole, sat down and drank a good amount of water. I sat there for an hour in the silence and watched the sun creep past the cave's upper edge and lower towards the horizon. The occasional hawk flew by, but otherwise it was as serene as I have ever known life to be.

I reached into my pack and drew out a pen and paper to write a letter home about this scene. My adjectives did not do the moment justice, but I felt the need to share it with my friends and family so many miles to the east in the urban sprawl. I took photos, but it would be weeks before that roll of film was finished and developed. After I had written the last word, I shoved my thumb deep into the fine red soil and left "my mark" on the page. Beneath the thumb print I quickly scrawled, "From the Red Centre", sealed the envelope and put it in my pocket.

I sat there in the timeless void and understood how this would be the perfect place for the nuns. It was inherently peaceful and spiritual and even evoked emotion. There were no outside influences, just an endless landscape and the sound of one's own thoughts. Pure peace.

Ultimately, the real world returned in the form of a voice from the top of the ladder. The doctor had completed his tasks and it was time to go. I reluctantly passed my backpack up and climbed the ladder, leaving the subterranean calm to walk back to my waiting Cessna.

My departure that late afternoon was picturesque. The sun was setting low on the horizon and the swarming hawks were beginning to settle. As I lifted off and retracted the wheels, the cliff face fell away below as if I were launching from an enormous stone aircraft carrier. I turned towards the sun and glanced back at the many openings where the birds now rested. And then there was one hole...slightly larger...a little foliage growing near the edge. It was the Nun's Cave and it was a place and a time that I would never forget.

***

When the Day is Young.

Outback Delivery.

6

THE ROAD LESS TRAVELLED

Airliner after airliner sat silent at the capital city airport, their pitot covers flapping limply in the occasional breeze. The light towers illuminated low patches of fog, adding to the ghostly setting of a tarmac filled with proud machines, but with no one to fly them. The entire nation was grounded; caught in the grip of an airline pilots strike.

Young charter pilots like me had never worked harder as we tried to take up the slack created by the industrial dispute. My home base of Kununurra was three stops and eight hours of flight time away, but for someone busily trying to fill their log book with multi-engine experience, that was heaven.

My Cessna 310 sat beyond the barbed-wire-topped fence, and the gate through which I had exited at Perth Airport the previous day was now locked. I scouted left and right until, in frustration, I hurled my knapsack over the fence and then followed it over myself. Of course, my trousers got hooked and ripped, but finally I was able to prepare my aircraft for the flight home.

The return leg was without passengers and there had been a severe temptation to sleep in and depart at a more leisurely hour. However, my company was waiting for the aircraft so that another pilot could fly another five miners south as soon as I returned. The temptation had been made even stronger as this had been the first night in months that I'd been away from the "outback" to a world that included suburbs, traffic lights and Kentucky Fried Chicken. Simple things for a simple bloke.

Even though I wore extra layers of clothing, I shivered in the darkness as the chill was a far cry from the hotter climate I had become accustomed to. Back home it was a constant dry heat that saw aircraft cabin heaters as a luxury at best and troublesome ballast at worst. Consequently, the heater in the Cessna had long been removed and the cockpit became very cold at altitude in these southern latitudes. Still, as the first rays of sun clipped over the horizon, I was nearly ready to depart and thought of the warmth I was flying to.

Spinning propellers and piston engines filled the jet void as we all lined up for our turn to depart. Runway 06 almost pointed straight into the rising sun and I squinted behind my sunglasses as I edged the throttles all the way forward and checked that the engines were producing the power I expected. With everything in order, I continued to speed down the runway until I lifted my Cessna into the sky and raised the wheels up into their wells.

The long nose of the aircraft sat in front, while either wing tip was characterised by huge, pointed, almond-shaped fuel tanks. With the two propellers now spinning in harmony, I surveyed the clean white wings and couldn't suppress the feeling that I was flying on a magic carpet. Only the chatter of air traffic control transferring me to the next frequency interrupted the peace of an early morning departure through still air.

Soon I was beyond the organised airspace of air traffic control and back in the world of map and compass. As I levelled off at 8,500 feet, the trees had merged into a broad green blanket which now began to tinge brown as I set course to the northwest. I filled out my log and managed my fuel surrounded by endless outback in every direction. The first stop was Meekatharra which sat around 400 miles and a little over two hours away; but there was no hurry.

The miles and minutes ticked by and I readied my charts and radios for the descent into Meekatharra. There were no passengers to brief for the arrival, so I just sat there waiting for the last few minutes before I would lower the nose of the Cessna and wind my way back to earth. Too easy.

Bang!

The aircraft slewed to the left and shook like it had driven onto a back road covered in rocks. I blocked the swinging nose of the aircraft by pushing on the right rudder pedal, but still the vibration continued to shake the aircraft to its core. I steadied myself and paused for a moment to assess what was actually creating this chaos. Scanning down the instruments, the gauges confirmed what my right rudder input was telling me; the left engine was the culprit. The flicking needles told me that the engine wasn't dead, but was having some type of sporadic seizure. Bang! Bang! Roar! Bang! Pop! Bang! The cacophony was not abating.

Speaking to myself all the while, I confirmed that the left engine had failed. I confirmed the appropriate levers that controlled the left-hand engine and set about shutting it down and putting it out of its misery. "Left throttle – closed", "Left pitch-feather, left mixture-idle cut-off". By closing these three levers I had stopped the engine, placed the stationary propeller edge-on to the airflow to minimise resistance to the slipstream and cut off the engine's fuel supply.

Things were now under control and the vibration had consequently ceased when the engine fell silent. Meekatharra was straight ahead as I pointed the nose down to descend and broadcast my situation and intentions to anyone in the area who would listen. The Cessna was flying nicely, so I returned to the troublesome engine and switched off its associated systems and considered if there was any need to access, or "cross feed", fuel from the left wing. With the airfield only minutes away, there was plenty of fuel still in the right wing.

Levelling off at the base of my descent, I increased the power on the right engine and squeezed the rudder pedal once again to keep the asymmetric aeroplane flying in a straight line. Another radio call met with no reply, so it seemed that I had the landing pattern to myself as I positioned to make my arrival. Check-check-check. "Don't do anything dumb now" I whispered.

In a conforming fashion I crossed the airfield at right angles, turned to track parallel to the runway and then turned once again back towards the runway for the final approach to land. Airspeed was of the essence as I made my final descent. Confident that I could glide to the runway, I selected the landing gear down. My speed was good and the runway now lay dead ahead. Aiming to land some distance down the runway, I began to lower the landing flaps in stages, and each time they took a bigger bite at the air mass that my lone engine was now pushing through.

With wheels and flaps extended and only a couple of hundred feet to descend, I reminded myself that I was now committed to land. There was no trepidation in my decision, just a realisation that the aircraft would struggle to initially climb away with only one engine operating and the wheels and flaps hanging down. *Keep it straight....keep on speed....not much further now. I'm down.*

I'd practised single-engine landings many times before, but this was the first one in earnest and fortunately it was a non-event. A full load of passengers would've made things a little more interesting. Between their added weight on board and explaining why that propeller wasn't turning anymore, I suspect that my workload would have doubled. As it was, the sky was clear and the drama was minimal. But it wasn't quite over yet.

After I parked the aircraft an engineer came over immediately, having seen my landing and taxi-in with one engine stopped. He popped the engine cowlings, pushed and prodded and then shook his head. One of the two magnetos had failed. The device responsible for supplying power to the spark plugs hadn't just ceased to function, its housing had failed. As a consequence, its inner workings had been left to spin and jam up and operate in anything but a regular manner. A straight failure would've been simple, leaving the second magneto to provide the spark, but in this case it had been a violent death.

The engineer wasn't shaking his head at the damage, but the fact that he was the only engineer in town. The others had headed to Perth where the pilots' dispute had created a flurry of work with top dollar being paid. It seemed that my Cessna was both well down the queue to be repaired and with no spare parts available in Meekatharra. Needless to say, my boss in Kununurra was rather upset as the aircraft had back-to-back bookings for the foreseeable future.

Within an hour, a company aircraft containing engineers and spare parts was winging its way over the 1,000 miles to repair my aeroplane. When the engineers arrived, they worked feverishly while I went searching for somewhere to eat in Meekatharra with its population of about 500 hearty folks. As I walked down the main street late that night, an old awning on a petrol station boasted of the "The Meekatharra Lubratorium" in faded, peeling paint. I was only a few hundred miles from the state's capital, but it was like another world.

I had not planned to have an engine failure or to be in a small country town for the night, but that was the nature of the job. And it is an aspect of being a pilot that I have always loved. Even in the airlines, when lives are routinely ruled by rosters and schedules, things can change at a minute's notice, introducing new places and interesting people. So often, aviation can ease us away from the highways in the skies to venture down the road less travelled.

***

7

THE SIGNPOSTS OF THE SKY

It is dead calm over the Pacific as the Boeing 747 cuts its way through the night. Los Angeles is still six hours away and our giant airliner is passing through the Intertropical Convergence Zone (ITCZ), or the "doldrums" as it was referred to by the sailors of old. It is a region where weather can be docile or violent and change from one to the other with very little warning. But tonight, as we sit seven miles above the earth, the moon is bright and the radar sweeps the horizon without a single cloud "painting".

In these small hours, conversation is often sporadic on the flight deck. There is little energy for enthusiasm and every shred of concentration is called upon to remain focused on the task while 400 people sleep silently in the darkened cabin. One eye scans outside while the other watches the miles slowly count down on the flight management computer. It's all very routine. And then something in the distance catches the eye.

Leaning forward, I rest my chin atop the instrument panel and attempt to shield its glow with my forearm. My eyes slowly adapt to the darkness outside and with the help of the moon I begin to see them: towering, pencil-like clouds, seemingly no wider than the aircraft itself. Like a sparse forest of white branchless trees they climb high into the sky and well above the level we are cruising at.

We call up San Francisco on the radio and obtain permission to weave left and right around these massive beanstalks. Still there is nothing painting on our weather radar, perhaps their girth is too slender to detect. Regardless, their vertical extent suggests rising currents that would give our jet a decent shake and our passengers quite a wake-up call, so we continue, left then right in the clear air. I ponder the consequences of flying through one of these pillars on a moonless night. Undoubtedly it happens and is probably attributed to "Clear Air Turbulence" in the absence of any radar evidence.

These tall, silent clouds are a far cry from the fierce rumbling demons of a storm front. They are deep, black monstrosities that flash light from within to display their brawn for hundreds of miles. These beasts turn the radar red as pilots steer their aircraft many miles off track to seek safe passage. These walls of turbulence and water have chewed aircraft up and spit them out. And yet, as a young charter pilot, my comrades and I would do our best to step safely between the lightning and thunder without a weather radar to guide us. I look back on those memories and recognise that fortune can sometimes favour the clueless.

Those same sailors that sailed the doldrums, cast their eyes to the horizon and looked for clouds to predict the coming weather, "Red sky at night, sailors delight..." So it is for aviators as they transit the skies, seeking out telltale clues of otherwise-invisible turbulence or wind shifts with varying altitude. Calm mornings and blanketing fog can spell disruption for airline timetables, but for the pilot it is evidence of a stable high-pressure system and a beautiful day once the fog clears.

A seemingly docile band of cloud at altitude can actually lie on the underside of a "jetstream". These ribbons of air can rush at speeds well over 100 miles per hour and can be a great friend or villainous foe depending upon your direction of passage. Either way, that docile band is a landmark in the sky, signalling strong winds above and a potentially rough ride until the aircraft is surfing in the jetstream's core. Strangely, despite its velocity, the core frequently provides the smoothest of rides for pilots and passengers.

The high wisps of cirrus clouds that resemble mares' tails in the sky are often the precursor to a frontal change, while a green tinge to frontal cloud brings the very real threat of hail. Grey nimbostratus clouds spell the death knell for visual flight and bring a real set of challenges for those who fly on instruments. That being said, on top of the cloud layer a different world can exist. Crystal clear skies, with a blanket of white below as far as the eye can see. And the "rush" of the cloud-tops as the aircraft emerges into that sunny world is an event pilots never tire of. For clouds also offer a sensation of speed that can only otherwise be obtained in the nap of the earth, where the terrain is unforgiving. At altitude there is the ability to speed down white valleys and wheel about bubbling alabaster towers of moisture with absolute freedom. These moments are when flying truly feels like flying and one can relate to John Gillespie Magee Jr. when he wrote those words, "Put out my hand and touched the face of God",

Despite the fact that such joy is to be found, clouds can also be the enemy. Those same harmless cumulus clouds can contain rocky ridges, or even another aircraft. Cloud can lurk at the bottom of an instrument approach and then thrash rain against the windscreen in the final stages of landing. Cloud can wrap ice around an aircraft and squeeze the lifeblood of airspeed from its veins. Cloud can toss a giant of the sky about as if it is a mere bottle bobbing on the ocean's waves. Cloud can creep in behind you and cordon off valleys, leaving no way out.

The air we fly through is magical. It is an invisible medium that flows by our wings and is mysteriously transformed into lift. Only when the environmental conditions intervene can we see the very substance that we depend upon for flight. The invisible fluid takes form as a strip of vapour from our wingtips in a turn, or grows into a thunderstorm with enough water within to flood a country town. In either form, it is only then that the air shows its face above the earth.

Without clouds the atmosphere is a maze of burbling air and strong currents waiting to bounce our tiny airframes about or push them through the sky at extreme speeds. Yet visible moisture, be it friendly and white, low and grey, fierce and black, or even green, tells us what may lie ahead in the next hundred miles, or the next few days. Clouds can work with us or against us, but it is still our eyes' only indicator in the visible sea above the earth. In so many ways they are signposts of the sky.

***

8

Landing Gear Down....
Or Is It?

The pilot and the plane could not have been more different. The vintage Cessna 310 was decades old and showing its age. The short nose and basic blue-and-white paint scheme echoed an era when aircraft ownership was heralded from brochures featuring happy families and picnic baskets. Inside, the old upholstery and yellowing curtains were not quite so romantic, nor was the twine glued to the control yoke to provide a grip in lieu of the long-perished rubber. Still, for the purpose of flight training, the old girl would do the job.

By contrast, the pilot under instruction this day was sharp down to the smallest detail. A crisply ironed uniform, shiny shoes and a clipped moustache, "Freddo" stood six-foot-something with a back as straight as a gun barrel. He had studied the handling notes and completed the written examination on the old Cessna and now he readied himself for the flight component of the licence endorsement.

Starting one engine, then the other, the aircraft chugged into life before she settled into a smooth rhythmic hum. Freddo checked every instrument meticulously and logged the pertinent numbers and times on a sheet of paper on the knee-pad that was strapped to his thigh. Before too long, all of the checks were completed and the engines were warmed up, with their indicating needles sitting comfortably "in the green". It was time to take to the sky.

The houses surrounding the airport fell away as the wheels were retracted and the Cessna climbed into the sky. The large almond-shaped fuel tanks on the tips of the wings dominated the view to either side while a broad centre stanchion divided the outlook through the windscreen ahead. The houses slowly petered out into green paddocks and the occasional row of farm sheds, and it was here that we would begin the range of exercises to familiarise Freddo with his new mount.

Initially, we subtly wheeled about the horizon, noting the aircraft's attitude in the turn. We then flew with a range of power settings and speeds to explore the performance of the aeroplane and how this changed the attitude and "trim" of the Cessna. There was hardly a cloud in the sky and even the wind was of the gentlest wafting nature. With an experienced pilot in the other seat, the flight was moving along smoothly. Just a few more handling exercises, a number of engine failures and then back to the circuit for some takeoffs and landings. It was all very standard stuff for a very standard aircraft type check-out.

After climbing even higher, we levelled off, completed more checks and slowed the aircraft to its minimum flying speed. We continued to reduce our speed even further and Freddo gently raised the aircraft's nose in an effort to maintain a constant altitude. In doing so we were allowing the smooth airflow over the wing to reach the point where it would break down and the Cessna would stall. At this time the aircraft lightly buffeted to the backdrop of a squawking warning horn before it gently pitched its nose down to gain airspeed and reinstate the airflow.

After a few more stalls I advised Freddo that we would examine a stall with the flaps lowered and the wheels extended to simulate an approach to land. Dutifully he slowed the aircraft to the appropriate speed and lowered an initial stage of flap from the trailing edge of the wing. Then, confirming that his speed had decreased sufficiently, he grasped the handle for the landing gear and selected it to the "down" position. The electric motor whirred audibly as the wheels began their journey and then began to lower...

Bang!

We looked at each other and then back at the bulb that indicated that the landing gear was extended. It had flashed momentarily, but now remained ominously dark. As Freddo continued to fly the aeroplane, I reached over and pressed on the light and it illuminated without hesitation, but extinguished as soon as I released the pressure. I now knew that the bulb had not blown and that the problem most likely lay in the landing gear. We cycled the landing gear up and down again, but the problem failed to go away. I looked at our fuel stocks and we had enough to keep us airborne for some hours still, so there was no need to rush into any plan of action.

At this time, the training flight became value added for Freddo. I resolved to carry out the emergency landing-gear extension procedure and, as there were two of us; we could literally do it from the book. I pulled the manual from the seat pocket and began reading through the procedure step by step. After basic troubleshooting we set about unlocking the manual gear extension handle and preparing to wind the wheels down. The procedure spoke of continuing to wind the handle for a couple of turns further once the "gear down" light had illuminated; but it never did.

Having exhausted our procedural options, I took over control of the aircraft and endeavoured to use the apparent force of gravity to my advantage. I pulled the Cessna into a series of tight turns that forced me down into my seat under the g-force but again this failed to have any effect upon the errant landing gear. It appeared that we were going to have to return to the airport for a landing with the status of the undercarriage still a mystery. Further complicating our cause was the fact that this was a very early model Cessna 310 and as a consequence it only possessed a single light to indicate whether the wheels were safely down or not. Later models had three individual lights that enabled the pilot to troubleshoot which one of the three undercarriage legs was the problem. We had no such luxury.

I had flown a range of models of the 310 over the years and scratched my head for an answer. I reviewed what I knew about the aircraft systems and then cross-checked the manual in front of me. The emergency extension hadn't worked, nor had the steep turns and g-force, and I was out of options. I double-checked our fuel status and general well-being and, outside of the undercarriage problem, all was well with the world.

We circled about the training area a little longer to both confirm that we had tried everything and to allow us time to secure loose items and sharp edges in preparation for a "gear collapse" on landing. I thought through various options with time and altitude at my disposal before committing to return to the earth. At this time I looked at the engines either side of me as they were bound to suffer extensive damage as their propeller blades struck the ground.

For the first time, the aeroplane's age may hold an advantage. Each engine was equipped with a two-bladed propeller rather than the more modern three-bladed style. If I could get those propellers to the horizontal position prior to touchdown, then perhaps they didn't have to strike the runway's unforgiving asphalt. It was a course of action that I might not explore if I was flying alone, but I had a commercially licensed flight instructor in the other seat.

We discussed the possibility and came to agreement that I would shut the engines down in the very last stage of the approach to land. As I focussed on landing the aeroplane, Freddo would use the starter motor nudge the propellers to the horizontal position and hopefully clear of striking the ground. The plan was now in place.

For the first time we advised Air Traffic Control of our predicament and co-ordinated a response from the control tower. In the first instance I would fly past the control tower so the controllers could examine the landing gear from outside the aeroplane. Following their inspection I would complete the final checks and position the Cessna to land, treating the landing gear as unsafe in all cases.

As I lined up to make the pass of the control tower, I was very conscious not to get distracted and fly too low or too close to the tower, thereby turning an undercarriage issue into something far greater. With the flaps down and the wheels hopefully lowered, I slowly passed the control tower, offering a gentle bank away so that the controllers could grab a slightly better view of my under-side. Wings back to level, I climbed away back into the circuit area.

Their findings were inconclusive. "It all looks good from here" were their words, but still the darkened undercarriage indicator stared at me. I acknowledged the tower's observations but requested that they prepare for an unfavourable outcome nonetheless. Accordingly, they cleared the airspace, runways and taxiways of any other aircraft and placed the fire trucks and emergency services on standby. I briefed Freddo one last time and we both tightened our harnesses a little more. For the second time the runway came into view dead ahead, but this time I was going to land.

Flying down the final approach was just like any other landing, although I was aiming a little further into the runway to allow for shutting down the engines at the last moment. With the airspeed steady, the airfield's perimeter fence slipped beneath me as I shut down both engines and selected the fuel selectors to "off". The black runway and its white central stripes now filled the windscreen and I focused solely on the landing. Outside my peripheral vision, Freddo kicked over the propellers before switching off all of the electrical power. The twin-engined Cessna was almost eerily quiet as we whistled down towards the runway.

The first touch on the main landing gear was smooth and we began to roll along the ground without event. I continued to fly the aircraft with the nose off the runway until it began to slow even further at which time I gently lowered the nosewheel to the ground. We were down on all three wheels and rolling along nicely. For the first time, it now seemed as though the event was a false alarm. A split-second after that thought crossed my mind, the old Cessna began to lean to the right as the undercarriage leg evidently began to give way under the weight.

At first I squeezed the left rudder pedal to keep the aircraft straight along the runway's centre-line, but as we slowed even further and the wing dipped lower it became obvious that my efforts would ultimately be in vain. As the wing went further down, the nose was raised in sympathy and a scraping noise started to emanate from behind me. I eased off the pressure on the rudder pedal allowing the aircraft to leave the runway towards the grass verge beside it.

Almost at a standstill, the right wing-tip dragged on the grass and kicked up a puff of dust before the whole airframe finally lurched to a reluctant halt. I checked that all of the switches and selectors were off before opening the door and exiting the aeroplane which now sat with a decided list to starboard. The trailing edge of the wing was only inches off the ground and it was only a small step to the ground and then a brisk walk away from the aeroplane just in case.

A fire truck pulled up nearby with its hose and foam at the ready while another vehicle with flashing lights stopped next to Freddo and me. Soon a circle of people surrounded the aeroplane and it was deemed to be safe from fire, although closer inspection indicated that the extended left landing gear was not locked down either. Over the next hour, a truck raised the wayward wing and the engineers set about making the undercarriage safe for the aircraft to be towed. It seemed that the grand total of damage was a scraped fibreglass tail-cone and grass stain to the right-hand tip-tank.

Freddo was still patting me on the back that evening when we had our first beer, but still I ran through the day's events trying to second-guess my actions. Pilots all tend to be their harshest critics and I was no exception. All in all I was happy with the outcome. Freddo moving the propellers to the horizontal undoubtedly prevented at least one "prop strike", but I doubt I would have done this if I was flying on my own.

Shutting down the engines was another decision I questioned, as it meant that I was committed to landing. Again, the runway and taxiways were clear of aircraft that could get in our way so there was not really anything that could force me to go around at that late stage of the approach. Even so, being committed to land at low level was nothing new as this was always the case on approach with either engine shut down. Ultimately, I ticked all of the boxes in my own mind.

Over the ensuing years, I always read the reports of Cessna 310s that had experienced undercarriage problems. Some were similar and some were totally unrelated. In our case it transpired that an electrical relay had become stuck when Freddo selected the landing gear down, causing the extension process to over-run and shear through the mechanical stops that would normally result in the wheels being locked down. The subsequent damage also rendered the manual extension of the landing gear to be ineffective. Despite any procedures or tight turns we could try, the landing gear was never going to lock down.

At the time, I was still a relatively young pilot and, like all out-of-the-ordinary flights, there was much to learn and today I am still learning. Many of the considerations back then in the tired old Cessna are still relevant in a glistening new Boeing. Fuel offers time and options, so don't rush down the wrong path prematurely. Use all of the options, services and people available to you. Always maintain an appreciation of the "big picture" and don't become transfixed with the minor emergency; altitude, like fuel, is your friend. And no matter what happens, always fly the aeroplane.

In aviation, you never know it all, and to think that you do is a dangerous attitude. Every time that I fly I appreciate that the gift of flight defies gravity and takes me away from the earth and into Mother Nature's realm. The only way that any pilot can continue to thrive and survive in that world is through respect of the surroundings, the machine and the magic of flight.

Sadly, Freddo was lost only a few years later when his aircraft plunged into the ground after takeoff. He was one of my best friends and a very talented pilot. Still, when we leave the security of the ground, nothing less than total respect for our privileged place in the sky will see us safely home.

Rest in peace mate.

***

9

ON THE RUN

"Be careful, you could get bloody killed up there," were my father's first words when I told him that I was to fly to New Guinea. His point was valid as many an aviator had come to grief amidst the short sloping runways and the towering mountaintops that lurked in the clouds. Anyway, it was just a delivery flight. However, there was irony in my father's words as he had been in New Guinea as a 19-year-old with a rifle and a bayonet. He had fought in those same jungles and could've been "bloody killed up there" too.

In retrospect his advice was both wise and foreboding, as in the next month I had enough drama to last a career, both on the ground and in the air. Although it was not surprising and the warning signs were there from the moment that this trainee pilot walked into my office. Ryan's family had recently purchased and rejuvenated a late model Piper Aztec with two overhauled engines and six newly upholstered seats inside. As an aging aeroplane went, this one was in very good condition.

What Ryan omitted to tell me in the first instance was that much of the work had been carried out after he had run off the end of the runway during his training on the aircraft. He had been disgusted with his previous instructor for letting it happen and for milking money without his training advancing. After some enquiries, I discovered that I knew the instructor and he was a pilot of the highest standards. He advised me to "watch out" as this was all an accident waiting to happen. My second warning, but for some reason I still persisted.

Ryan was a rather average pilot, but I gathered he was a very well-connected and proficient salesman. He spoke at a million miles per hour and much of it had two meanings. However, he was no fool. It was 1991 and he was telling me that the day would come when a business could be run by a computer small enough to fit a brief case and a "mobile" phone. I laughed at the thought and suggested that he focus on his flying. He did focus on his flying and I endorsed him to fly the Aztec over a very busy month of training.

On completion of the flight he approached the owner of my company to permit me to fly to New Guinea with him to deliver the aircraft. I was keen to go and I gather that my boss was well remunerated. Still, the departure was planned for the next week and I didn't have a valid passport, although Ryan assured me that I only need a "General Declaration" for a ferry flight and it had been taken care of. And indeed it had.

Our flight north from Sydney was without issue, although Ryan had purchased two crates of signal flare guns amongst many other items. Much later he quietly told me that the flare guns' plastic barrels could be replaced with metal piping in New Guinea and were a useful means of defence. Full of fuel and freight and inspected by customs, we left Australian shores from Cairns and pointed our nose towards New Guinea.

We paralleled Cape York and crossed the Torres Strait to make landfall and clear customs at the small port of Daru, thus avoiding the congestion of the busy Port Moresby Airport. However, it became apparent that politics were in play when we met with the New Guinea authorities who promptly wanted to impound our aircraft despite the paperwork being in order. Ryan informed me that this was merely an extortion attempt to elicit funds from his father and nothing more. I was not quite as confident as I finished refuelling the Aztec and walked to the nearby customs office.

Ryan was insistent that we had to get to Port Moresby and "his people" no matter what and kept muttering this under his breath. He looked at the short official in uniform escorting us, the aeroplane and then the drink machine at the entrance to the offices. He then requested that we be excused to gather some coins from the Aztec to purchase a couple of cold drinks.

As soon as we made it back to the aircraft he whispered, "Let's go!" I was at a loss, as we hadn't settled the administrative issue nor had we paid the refuelling agent. Nevertheless, we were on his turf in his aeroplane so I burst the Aztec into life and set off at speed for the runway's end, completing my checks as I went. As I advanced the throttles, the refueller gave up the chase and I caught a glimpse of his disbelief as we roared by and took off. The sun was setting lower, but fortunately Jackson Field at Port Moresby was one of the few airports in New Guinea where night operations were possible. Even so, as we flew into the night across the Gulf of Papua I was well aware of the towering ranges that sat in the darkness out to our left.

The control tower at Jackson Field was not fazed by our unannounced arrival and soon we were parking near the local aero club which sat in total darkness. Ryan's "people" were there to meet us with smiles and congratulatory handshakes for our "escape" from Daru. However, they bundled us into a car and drove at speed to our lodgings as a night curfew had recently been put in force due to a spate of lawlessness. As we sped down the road, I watched as two local men sawed through the hose of a bowser at a petrol station and three others brawled nearby. Soon we drove through the razor-wire-topped fence of our compound and finally had the opportunity to catch our breath.

The long day's flying and the excitement had exhausted me. I slept deeply that night, only stirring when the light began to pour through the verandah windows where I was lying. That morning we revisited the aircraft which, to my horror, now had its doors and lockers sealed with customs tape and a notification that the Aztec was impounded by Customs. Ryan and his father laughed at my concern as this problem could be resolved much more cheaply than if the aeroplane had been held prisoner at Daru.

We retired to the Aero Club for a soft drink and I caught up with one of my former students who was now a fully-fledged pilot with one of the local operators. I listened intently to his advice as *he* was now the instructor, and he steered me towards an old chap sitting quietly in the corner. The man's white hair had a decided wave in it and his moustache was shaped like that of a fighter pilot of old. In many ways, it seemed that when World War Two ended this gentleman had simply chosen to stay in-country. And perhaps he had.

Although I had quite some hours in my log book, I realised that flying in New Guinea was of a very different nature. I sat down with this white-haired gent and endeavoured to glean any knowledge that I could from his obvious years of experience in this challenging environment. After a long conversation he summed it up very, very simply. "If you're flying under visual flight rules, stay visual. If you're flying under instrument flight rules, stay on instruments. Confuse the two and you'll kill yourself." That phrase "kill yourself" had surfaced again, this time from a total stranger. I bought him another drink, thanked him and then excused myself to return to my hosts.

When I sat down they congratulated me once again on my daring escape, about which I was feeling decidedly uncomfortable. When I asked them about my return flight to Australia, they smiled and advised me that my boss had authorised for me to stay and supervise

Ryan on a number of flights around their network before I would be going home. I mentally gulped with a tinge of frustration at not having been consulted, but it appeared that I was now here for a longer haul.

Unbelievably, two days later our first flight would transit Daru. I nervously protested, fearing that there was a bounty on my head and a refueller with a machete to grind. Again I was laughed at as that issue had been "resolved", and indeed it had. When I landed at Daru, both the fuelling agent and the official smacked me on the back in jest, smiling and pointing. "You're cheeky. You're so cheeky", they kept repeating, mimicking the Aztec soaring into the skies with their hands. It seemed that all had truly been forgiven and I self-consciously smiled back.

From Daru we flew to Balimo, a small village near the Fly River that would serve as our base over the coming weeks. Its short grass runway was a welcome sight after Daru and the remote location was a breath of fresh air after Port Moresby. We rode in the back of a jeep to our lodgings and passed a group of nurses outside what I guessed to be a mission or hospital. They all waved and smiled broadly and amongst their warm brown faces was one pale white face with bright red hair.

Our lodgings were simple. A small but modern cabin built by the swampy edge of the lagoon system with all manner of birdlife moving about in abundant numbers. I wandered about the cabin and breathed in this untouched setting of flora and fauna, smiling at the local villagers and content not to return to Port Moresby. As I stood outside, its perfection was only tinged when Ryan called out to warn me of the abundance of crocodiles lurking in the waters nearby.

It was time for dinner, so I retreated inside for a meal of rice cooked over a portable gas burner. I devoured it quickly and lay down in the darkness to listen to the orchestra of insects and squawking birds outside. It was a cacophony of sound, yet still it was relaxing like a lullaby. This was the sort of flying that I loved, away from the hustle and bustle. My earlier reservations began to slip away as sleep closed in. After a dubious arrival in New Guinea, I now wished that I could stay and fly about this natural beauty for weeks to come. Sometimes you should be careful what you wish for.

***

10

CLOSE CALLS

I was still in the dark about the true purpose of our flight. I overheard muffled conversations about local elections and natural resources, but nothing that I could comprehend and even less that I was privy to. On most sectors we carried gentlemen that were obviously held in high esteem in the various villages, but I never came to know who they were. From my perspective, I was to observe if Ryan was competent to fly this "network", but as the days passed it became increasingly obvious that I was there as the primary pilot.

Our first flight was to Lake Murray and it was a short, simple one under crystal blue morning skies. While my passengers made their way to the village to conduct their business, I stayed with the aircraft and reviewed the next sector to Kiunga. Kiunga was the only airport so far, other than Port Moresby, that possessed a serviceable radio beacon and the means for making an approach to land in cloud. It was a promising discovery, although I did note the warning on the airport chart of the proximity to the Indonesian border which fighter jets patrolled.

When my passengers arrived there was lively discussion and I heard apparent offers of another aircraft with "Spirit of Lake Murray" painted on its flanks. I don't know if that ever eventuated, but it was an offer I heard repeated at most ports of call. Some of the local villagers seemed excited at the concept and some seemed a little angered. One villager kindly gave me a bundle of fresh fish and this was the true, generous face of New Guinea that I came to treasure.

As we lifted off from Lake Murray, the flight time to Kiunga was a mere 40 minutes. The blue skies now had the occasional fluffy white cumulus cloud and, although harmless, they seemed to be growing as I watched them. I had seen brewing storms in the outback and this was very similar, but very much quicker. The cloud tops were bubbling like froth from a badly poured beer. Now there was another cloud…and another. And now there was a heavy shower to the right, to the left and one ahead of me. I descended a little and manoeuvred left and right to remain clear of the heavy downpours that now emerged from the base of the clouds.

In 15 minutes the weather had changed dramatically and my options were shrinking as the rain began to beat on the windscreen and I peered through the Perspex. I was contemplating descending even further to try and weave my way to Kiunga when a cold chill ran up my back. I looked at my reducing altitude in diminishing visibility and heard the old pilot's warning from the Aero Club days: "If you're flying under visual flight rules, stay visual. If you're flying under instrument flight rules, stay on instruments. Confuse the two and you'll kill yourself."

With those words in my head I advanced the throttles and climbed to the published safe altitude, thankful that Kiunga had a beacon to home in on in these days before GPS. Clear of the ground and enveloped in cloud I felt far more at ease and in another 15 minutes the line of clouds dissipated and Kiunga lay dead ahead.

Similar to Lake Murray, our visit was met with a mixed response by the local villagers, and so it was for the entire day as we looped around the Southern Highlands and back to Balimo. On the final leg to Balimo one of our dignitaries pointed to an airstrip below and I was asked to land there. I overflew the grass strip which was situated on a river's edge and surrounded by tall trees. It didn't look terribly long, but long enough nonetheless.

I flew the Aztec down and lined up on the runway with a howling crosswind from my left. I locked my gaze on the near edge of the field and drove the aeroplane towards it at the slowest possible safe speed. When the wheels hit I retracted the flaps quickly and dumped the lift they created, transferring our weight more onto the wheels. I asked the brakes for all that they had to offer and came to a halt with a little room to spare before turning back to where a crowd had gathered.

Once again the conversation was lively, but this time I was far from idle as my passengers debated their case. I paced out the runway and calculated how much distance was needed to depart and at my current weight it would be a close thing. The strong crosswind didn't offer any assistance and I sweated on what I was to do. In the middle of my internal debate, my group arrived back with an additional very large passenger who obviously had some standing in the community. This takeoff was going to be right on the very limits.

As I lined the Aztec up as close to the fence as I dared, I straightened the nosewheel and sat there for a moment. The crosswind had now swung slightly on the nose which would assist us in getting airborne. I said a silent prayer that if I got away with this I would never do anything so dumb ever again and I then brought the throttles to full power and held the Aztec on its brakes. It buffeted about like a bronco waiting to be sprung loose from the bullpen until I released the brakes and set the aeroplane free.

I mushed back in my seat under the acceleration and we were off to a good start. The runway bounced beneath me and the needle on the airspeed indicator seemed to take forever to rise to a satisfactory speed. All at once the runway end loomed large, the airspeed was sufficient, and the feel of the control wheel told me the Aztec was ready to fly. I eased her into the air and retracted the wheels as soon as the runway was a memory. The perimeter fence flashed beneath us and I rolled slightly to the right to follow the river in an effort to accelerate. Altitude was optional at this point, but speed was mandatory.

Ultimately, I gained both and climbed the Aztec away from the unforgiving terrain and into the sky before handing control over to Ryan. He flew us home as I stared out the window with a mix of relief and self-recrimination. It was too close for my liking and I vowed to never feel pressured into exercising poor judgement ever again.

That evening the Balimo villagers gathered up small fish, prawns and eels trapped in the reeds by the ebbing tide. Cooked over the gas burner with boiled rice it was a cherished feast for my exhausted body and soul. That night I fell asleep as the sun set and once again slept the most restful sleep I had known. I was only woken at one point by the yelping of a dog being taken by a crocodile not far from the cabin. It was a heinous sound, but I was too weary to care and far too hesitant to go outside.

The next day called for a number of stops and a return to Port Moresby for the night. As I inspected the aircraft that morning I discovered a small hole in the lower and upper engine cowlings that resembled the marks of a small calibre bullet. I wondered if one of the previous day's discussions had been more heated than I had realised. It was minimal damage, but still struck me as strange and left me grasping for an alternate cause.

Midway through our flight we were scheduled to land at Moro on the edge of Lake Kutubu. I had very little information about the airport other than the fact that the runway was of a generous length. I had made several landings so far on runways still surfaced in sheets of clattering steel that were laid in World War Two, but I had no such knowledge of Moro's airstrip.

Approaching Moro, the weather started to close in, so I held my altitude above the clouds with little hope of locating my destination. My alternate plan was to simply carry on to Port Moresby and I was busy organising this when a large hole appeared in the cloud below. I could see that dark waters lay beneath and by my calculations that should be Lake Kutubu. I entered an orbit over the hole to confirm my suspicions before lowering a stage of flap from the wings and starting a gentle descending spiral clear of the cloud.

Down and down we continued, and I was about to abort my endeavour and climb away when I happened upon the low grey base of the cloud. Beneath the cloud the visibility was clear, but now I had to work out where on the lake I was situated. At low speed I tracked along the shore line waiting for any distinct feature that I could reconcile with the chart on my lap. Then there it was: A small headland bending around to the left. Based upon that information, a small island should lie ahead of me, and so it did.

I rounded the island and a small inlet and there sat the runway at Moro and by comparison it was huge! There was approach lighting and a hive of activity as large Russian helicopters slung loads beneath them and Southern Air Transport C-130s waited to depart. It was a metropolis in the wilderness with aircraft flying under all manner of flags. I was in awe of the operation and noted that as my passengers disembarked they were discussing a gas line running to the southern shore of New Guinea. Ever curious, I was to remain intrigued as once again I was ordered to stay with the aeroplane and wait obediently. I did so and watched the show in the sky about me as the clouds poured forth and then disappeared once again in a manner I was beginning to recognise.

Still a little unsettled by some of the conversations and the suspect hole in the aeroplane, I requested if I could obtain a passport when we returned to Port Moresby the next day. After all, I had only originally been asked to fly the aeroplane to New Guinea and not across its width and breadth. Ryan and my hosts were more than happy to take me to the Australian Consulate and the next day I had a new passport and significantly more peace of mind.

Over my remaining time in New Guinea, the flying was far more relaxed and in general I was undertaking the task I had been employed to do. Ryan and I flew north, south, east and west to all manner of airfields and took in all kinds of sights. There were airfields that possessed only one way in and one way out, down narrow valleys and runways so steep that you turned sideward after landing to prevent rolling back on your tail. We crossed Kokoda where the Australian troops had created their legend during the war and I had clambered over the remnants of a Mitchell bomber and Thunderbolt fighter at Girua, sensing the history with every touch. The Kokoda crossing had claimed many aircraft over the years, lured into the more obvious and inviting "False Gap". I made sure that I didn't fall for that mistake and on one crossing I flew as high over the mountains as I dared without oxygen.

We also revisited the Indonesian border, but this time at its southern tip. There, at Bensbach, sits a hunting lodge reminiscent of something one might find in "King Solomon's Mines". The large wooden buildings sat on pillars among the lush, lush jungle while the small clearing about the accommodation was frequented by deer in large numbers. The fishing too was beyond belief with Barramundi as large as I had ever seen and even tastier to eat.

Yet the most thought-provoking journey came when we crawled along New Guinea's western coast to Lae. It was here that my namesake, Flight Lieutenant "Frank" Owen Smith is buried, having been killed during the war. I was desperate to visit his grave, but unfortunately my driver misunderstood me and drove me to a native burial ground instead of the war cemetery. Out of time and with fading daylight, I failed to visit Frank's resting place. However, that day was not without significance as I wandered away from the confines of the airports we visited. It was only then that I truly appreciated how dense the jungle could be.

My father had related how, during the war, the enemy could be a matter of feet away, but you still would not be able to see them. Even though my father was never prone to exaggerate, I had always found such a statement difficult to comprehend. Yet, as I stood amongst the thick, tangled web of vines, I truly understood his words and wondered how young men could survive, let alone fight in this steaming nightmare. I also thought of the aircrew operating their aircraft out of muddied airfields with limited resources and the ever-changing weather pushing them down towards the jungle's canopy. Somehow they did.

From my first controversial landing at Daru to my anonymous departure on the big white airliner, my time in New Guinea had surpassed anything that I had foreseen. The people and places that I had encountered in the heartland enchanted me and seemed far removed from Port Moresby and the grubby politics that I perceived was taking place.

A simple delivery flight had transformed into an adventure full of lessons and a less-than-subtle reminder of my own limitations. I continue to hold the bush pilots of New Guinea in the highest regard as day after day they confront what I call challenges and they call routine. They are all very conscious of how quickly these skies can turn and bite, but still they criss-cross the inhospitable terrain without fuss. For me, that chapter of my career is characterised by the magnificent memories of the villagers, the landscape and my share of close calls.

***

Meeting the 'locals' in New Guinea.

A relic of New Guinea's wartime past.

11

A Tragic Loss

Miserable. Absolutely miserable.

The water beaded down the window of my office while the drops tapped on the roof overhead. The weather had grown progressively worse over the last couple of hours from merely low overcast to showers of rain and even lower patches of cloud. Student pilots gathered in groups, huddled around coffees and cups of soup as very little flying was bound to take place today. The clouds sat on the ranges to the west, preventing any navigational training, hanging too low for even more basic lessons to take place. My booking sheet had been wiped clean too with the exception of one flight. It was a cross-country flight in a twin-engined Beech Duchess aircraft to instruct a student on the ways of flight, with reference solely to instruments. I looked out the window again. This was just the day for that.

Lined up on the runway and ready for takeoff, drops of water ran down my neck from my soaked collar, and the student's flight plan had not escaped the rain unscathed either. Nevertheless, he advanced the throttles and we accelerated along the runway to the warble of the spinning propellers and the din of the thrashing raindrops on the windscreen. A few minutes after takeoff we punched into the belly of the clouds and weren't to see the ground for another hour when we flew our approach some miles away.

Over the next four hours, my student acquitted himself well in rather trying conditions and he could feel well pleased with himself. It was a sentiment I shared after the flight and before we packed up and headed home for a lazy Sunday evening indoors. The weather seemed to be improving again, so maybe tomorrow would be better.

The phone rang early the next morning and wouldn't stop for the rest of the day. The words, "One of your aircraft is missing..." quickly blew out any cobwebs that may have lingered from the night's slumber. In the first instance, I couldn't make sense of the news as I noted down the registration and reached for yesterday's bare flight-booking sheets. Self-doubt crept over me as I thumbed down the page. Everything and everyone was accounted for. In fact, the aircraft in question wasn't even listed, as it was cross-hired to another organisation at a different airfield. Then the penny dropped. It was our aircraft, but not flying out of our base. They had staged through our airfield in the preceding days, but the aircraft had been parked on the far side of the aerodrome.

As I began to grasp the situation fully, the fax machine started to spew out reams of paper. The first details were confusing. Despite being based elsewhere, the aircraft had departed from our airfield that previous morning, a short while before I had set course into the less than ideal weather. Furthermore, the aircraft had apparently been planning to fly visually across the ranges, which were obviously shrouded in low cloud.

What was known was that there were two young men on board. No flight plan had been submitted and the alarm had been raised the previous evening when they had failed to arrive at their destination. Nothing had been seen or heard of them since they had retracted their wheels on departure, and now they were somewhere along their 250-kilometre route which included some very inhospitable terrain.

By now, a fleet of aircraft, pilots and spotters were being organised to conduct a full-scale search for the missing aircraft and its occupants. Based on their fuel load, a potential search area was drawn up and then subdivided into smaller sectors for individual aircraft to scour. The weather was far friendlier now, but I reminded our pilots not to get caught up in the excitement and media hype that was beginning to erupt. One by one they were assigned an aircraft and a search area, and one by one they took to the skies.

With the aircraft on the way, I retired to my office and compiled a flight plan for my own assigned search area, well to the west of the ranges and south of the missing aircraft's planned destination. All the while I struggled with the thought of the low cloud and steep hills that would have confronted the young pilot and his passenger. Having flown that day, I found it hard to conceive that they had made it beyond the hills, but a disciplined search must cater for all possible options based upon the aircraft's ability to stay in the air for the maximum possible time.

It was a thought that was reinforced as I crossed the ranges on the way to the search area. Looking down between two functioning engines and from a safe altitude, there was still cloud on the ground in places, and elsewhere were ragged ravines and gnarly, jutting peaks. A chill went down my spine as I had force-landed an aeroplane in this very same area only three months before and I knew just how terrible the terrain could be. Ahead the sky was clear and the sun warmed the cockpit as my load of spotters and I continued onto our allocated patch of sky.

Overhead our search area, we flew a predetermined pattern that would cover every inch. Occasionally a charred tree or a dumped car glinting in the sun would cause a stir amongst the crew, but generally it was an uneventful process of elimination. I rigidly stuck to the flight plan and my crew kept their noses against the windows. Still, in the ensuing hours my mind would occasionally drift to the missing young men. Were they still alive? If not, what had they gone through in their final moments? If they were alive, where were they? Were we frustratingly flying over their heads? It was torturous for me to contemplate any eventuality, but any reality for them must have been far, far worse. I prayed for their well-being many times as I flew up and down the vacant paddocks.

Over the next few days the search continued in earnest as the skies cleared. The ranges seemed to still be the most likely site for the aircraft, should it have crashed or been forced down. Helicopters scoured the area at a lower level, while their fixed-wing counterparts flew tracks in the sky over larger surrounding areas. Both men were young and fit, but still, as each day passed, hope faded, little by little. A tragic outcome became increasingly more likely and the drop in morale amongst the search crews was tangible, but still they flew hour after hour until it was decided they would fly no more.

Although the official search drew to a close, every single aircraft that subsequently crossed those ranges was flown with one eye on the ground below. Charter pilots, flight instructors and students alike were all aware of the missing aircraft and continued to look for the lost fliers. Despite their efforts, the answer was not to be found from the skies. Three weeks later, on a sunny Sunday, a bushwalker sighted the burnt wreckage on the far side of a valley. On steeply sloping terrain it had crashed amidst towering trees whose foliage had obviously concealed the crashed aircraft from the air. The mystery had been solved, but it was not until the area was searched that the true extent of the tragedy was revealed.

The young pilot and his passenger were not found in the wreckage. They were found a couple of kilometres from the crash site where they had perished from the combined effects of exposure and the burns they had received on impact. They had apparently survived for a few days alone in the rugged bushland and that thought further disturbed me. Following the discovery of the aircraft and its occupants, the media's interest was rekindled and now photographs of their young faces filled the front pages of newspapers. This only exacerbated my frustration as I lay down each night. Frustration at how close the search aircraft must have been. Frustration at the age-old killer of high hills and low cloud. Frustration at their terrible end.

The investigation would subsequently report that the aircraft had been seen by bushwalkers operating normally and flying midway between the valley floor and the overcast that sat upon the tops of the ridges. Trying to weave their way through the ranges rather than over them, they had ultimately reached rising terrain that they flew into with the engine still producing power. As with any investigation's outcomes, one is left with a long series of "What ifs?"

The young pilot only had 100 hours of flight time and less than three hours on the type of the aeroplane that crashed that day. Combined with the poor weather and rugged terrain it was a lethal combination that has spelt the end for many in the past and, unfortunately, will most likely mean the same again in the future. It would seem that there was poor judgement displayed to depart in such weather and an attempt to navigate the mountain ranges visually, and much of the subsequent banter surrounded this thought. Still, there are very few old pilots that haven't exercised poor judgement on occasions as a young pilot. Fortunately, the majority have lived to learn and tell the tale.

Ultimately, we are the sum of all of our experiences. With every hour in the cockpit, near miss or tragedy that I have witnessed, I have learned a little more. And yet I still have so much to learn. The loss of those two young men on that mountain-range was a particularly sobering experience for me on so many levels. The fact that the crash site was so close to where I had been forced down touched a nerve, while working at a flying school I was surrounded by fresh enthusiastic faces. Would these keen young aviators all make it through? I guessed that only time would tell.

***

12

WHEN THE DAY IS YOUNG

The groan of the hangar door stirs the silence of the night. Closed and content it has no desire to open and allow the world outside to pour into its confines, for inside the small aeroplane is still sound asleep. However, the source of the disturbance stirred some time ago, called by the stillness of the air and the pinpoints of light twinkling in the sky above. It is time to fly.

There were no other vehicles on the back road to the airfield and the only other sign of life was the occasional rabbit that skipped across the narrow road. Inside the car the vapour climbed from the coffee that sat in its holder and the bag of charts and headsets sat "rode shotgun" on the passenger seat. For some, Sunday morning is a time for sleep and lazy risings. But not for all.

After unlocking and locking the aerodrome gates in the glare of the headlights, the car bumped along the grass clearing beside the long black strip of tar before parking in the shelter of the hangar's wall. Coffee cup and curled collar keep the chill at bay, but its bite is there every time skin touches the metal of padlocks, or the aircraft's wing.

The tyres resist the pull of the tow bar at first but in time relent. Perhaps the aeroplane also feels the cold but yields at the anticipation of the clearest of skies and calmest of air. Covers are removed, and checks are completed, each action edging the tiny aircraft closer to an active state. Finally, the feet upon its wing and the closing cockpit door signal that the time is close as the first glow of dawn reveals the peaked outline of the nearby hangar.

The clicking of the harness binds man and machine as the propeller flicks over and the lifeless dashboard dials shake into life. Digital displays speak of frequencies as the needles indicating the engine's health slowly climb from yellow to green. All the while the day grows increasingly brighter, revealing the detail of the rustic surrounding scene.

Shadows become trees and in time individual leaves can be seen. The windsock hangs limply and lifeless as a lone white bird scratches around its base. The runway, now liberated from darkness, stretches to the far end of the field with small pockets of mist floating at chest height. Above, the endless black yields to blue and the stars step back from centre stage.

The brake is released, and the aeroplane rolls effortlessly away from the hangar to the runway's edge. By now it is warm beneath its cowling and ready to respond to its pilot's hand easing up the throttle, calling for more power. Key to the left, key to the right and a small, smooth drop in energy confirms that the magnetos are also awake. Lever down and lever up and the subtlest of surges reveal the carburettor's compliance. All is ready and the silence on the radio is golden.

Turning onto the runway the strobe lights flash against the hangars that hold the last of the night's shadows. Ahead, the black strip narrows into the distance and begs for acceleration. The sky is clear, and the nearby hills are reflecting a spectrum of colours as the rays of light accentuate the shades of nature: greens, browns and yellows. A last look, a deep breath and a smooth push of the long black lever.

The spinning disc of the propeller becomes even more transparent as its revolutions increase. Biting into the air it drags the aircraft forward; then begins the gradually intensifying struggle with the earth's friction in the race to the runway's end. The rush of the air and the roar of rubber on tar fill the ears as the airspeed indicator's needle works its way clockwise on the dial's face. When the magic number is reached, the wings tell the pilot that the aircraft is finished with the earth with the subtlest of force easing through the control column and into the palm of the hand. The obedient pilot complies with a gentle rearward pull and gravity is put in its place.

The ground falls away and treetops slip beneath the windshield's edge. The horizon sits nestled on the tip of the aeroplane's nose and either side more and more blue sky fills the windows. The instruments confirm the science, but the world outside describes the magic of flight.

The first turn cuts through the virgin air and a glance back at the airfield confirms the hangars and runway are now in the past. The present is life in the three dimensions with the slightest touch yielding a freedom that is not available when anchored to the soil. Below, the township still slumbers with smoke rising from chimneys and cars silent in their driveways.

The roads are empty except for a lone truck loaded with newspapers, and block by block the streetlights extinguish for the day. The surface of a lake mirrors the sky above although a faint trail is carved by a flock of birds skimming the surface and lazily retracting their landing gear.

Time has no reference in these moments other than in the limits of the fuel tanks. To go here or there is neither here nor there. It is the joy of wandering rather than the mission of travel. These are the moments to cherish, to drink in without the pressure of everyday life. Sometimes they are stolen from the slumber hours, but the reward for that sacrifice is great.

Below, the tapestry of the planet is there for the pilot to study and contemplate and circle around to look over once more. There is no ticking clock or pressing deadline to compress the wonder. It is the freedom of flight that we fortunate few share with the birds. We can soar and survey the ever-changing scene from a privileged vantage point and breathe in the wonder of our world. For those who fly, the joy of the sky is always something to behold.

***

13

FLIGHT TO PARADISE

I was excited. From time to time, opportunities present themselves in aviation and this one was a real gem. A missionary organisation had purchased a newly refurbished aeroplane and now they wanted me to participate in the delivery flight. On its own that news was enough to pique my interest as the flight would be a change from the day-to-day of flight instruction and the occasional charter that my career had recently been providing me. However, there was more to this task as they wanted the aeroplane delivered to a small island paradise in Micronesia.

But well before I ever set foot on a crystal-white beach or peered into the aqua waters of Yap Island, the flight began to throw up challenges of a different kind. In fact, the challenges began with my first flight in the aeroplane!

As I had not flown the trusty old Britten Norman Islander before, I set about reading all of the manuals thoroughly before my check flight. I calculated figures regarding fuel, I memorised every number and airspeed that I could possibly need and worked every graph and table twice through. When it came time to fly the aeroplane, I strapped into the left-hand seat quite confident of the aeroplane's vital statistics; now I just had to fly it. Unfortunately, the check pilot beside me seemed a little unfamiliar with the Islander.

As I ran through the engine-start sequence, he seemed to follow my actions with a degree of uncertainty. In the air the story was the same, although he admitted to not having flown the twin-engined Islander for quite some time. This became blatantly obvious when he demonstrated shutting down an engine and sought to feed fuel to the operating engine from the tank in the opposite wing; this procedure is known as "cross-feeding".

With the propeller beside me stationary in the airflow and the right-hand engine roaring, he desperately searched for the fuel selector. He looked on the floor between our seats and on the centre pedestal below the throttles in front of us. Eventually I pointed up towards the fuel selectors on the roof and he embarrassingly acknowledged their presence. Personally, I was a little worried about what he'd been watching before takeoff as I completed my checklists.

I was eventually endorsed to fly the Islander, but the aeroplane that was to cross the Equator was still sitting in the hangar. Recently painted in a shining red-and-white scheme, it was being fitted with huge metal tanks to carry the additional fuel needed for the long overwater crossing. As I wandered around the aircraft, I discussed in detail the modified fuel system with the engineers who had designed it. It had been approved by the aviation regulatory body and consisted of a series of levers mounted on a panel that would in turn cycle the relevant valves.

As so often is the case, the fuel selector panel was primitive in appearance but would prove effective in its operation. The panel would be on the floor. As for fuel-quantity gauges, the system would date back to the earliest studies of fluid dynamics. There would not be any dials or electrical sensors, simply clear hoses running down the front of the forward tanks behind the pilots' seats. As they were filled with a known quantity, the hoses would be marked with a thick black pen to reflect the corresponding level and quantity of the fuel contained in the tanks.

As I recalled my high school physics lessons and contemplated this seemingly overly-simple system, I received a tap on the shoulder. The gentleman introduced himself as "Rick" and he was a senior pilot with the missionary organisation and would be flying with me to Yap Island. Rick was an experienced pilot in his own right and had significant experience on the Britten Norman Islander. He had also undertaken a good deal of preparation for the flight.

Over the next few days we both pored over the charts that would see us fly to the northern tip of Australia, around New Guinea to Manus Island and across the Pacific to Yap. With the ferry tanks full of fuel, we would be over the regular flying weight for an Islander, something that the regulator had approved for the ferry flight. As a consequence it would be unwise to attempt to fly over the towering jungle ranges, particularly considering that the aircraft would undoubtedly be heading down in the case of an engine failure.

On a positive note, Rick had recently purchased a newly released GPS unit. I had read about these sophisticated navigational devices, but had only ever seen one previously. It was about the size of a hardback book with a small aerial the size of your thumb connected to the body by a cable. Rick explained how it would sit on the dashboard and instantly display our position as latitude and longitude, our speed over the ground and even whether we were left or right of our flight-planned track. We didn't need any navigational beacons on the ground sending out a homing signal as this GPS was fully self-contained. Amazing!

Rick's toys, experience, enthusiasm and preparation for the flight bolstered my confidence and each day we watched the Islander's systems reach completion. There were more engine runs, test flights and fine tuning but finally the aircraft was complete, certified and ready to transit the Southern Hemisphere on its long haul northward. We stowed our life raft and emergency equipment in easily accessible locations, leaving just enough room for us each to carry one bag. We then tucked the aircraft in for the night, planning to make an early start the next day.

Rick and I were happy with the weather forecast for our first day. Despite some early morning fog patches and a little low cloud around the Sydney basin, the skies were forecast to be clear. From Bankstown we would head north for about 900 nautical miles to Townsville on a flight that would take around eight hours in the slow but steady Islander. The boxy-looking twin-engined aeroplane possessed a high wing atop the fuselage and landing gear that was fixed down in the airflow. It was an aircraft that was designed to fly safely at low speeds and operate into and out of very short runways. It was a task that it performed admirably, but the downside was a virtual dawdle when flying between two points.

It was an ideal first sector as it was over land and offered a great opportunity to monitor the aeroplane's performance and fuel consumption prior to the long overwater legs. Furthermore, should there be any maintenance issues; we would be able to have them addressed at Townsville. And very early on in the flight it appeared that there may be a couple of issues.

Firstly, as we departed Sydney we levelled off in a bank of the low cloud that had been forecast. It was a cool May morning and while the airframe remained clear of ice forming on the wings, the engines began to run a little rough as if ice was beginning to form in the narrow channel within the carburettor. Immediately I selected "Carburettor Heat" to redirect warm air into that section of both engines but, despite having functioned before take-off, one lever was jammed stiff. The right engine continued to run roughly, so our best solution was to climb clear of the cloud's moisture, which we did satisfactorily. However, now oil began to seep along the side of the left engine cowling outside my window.

I checked the gauges and the oil quantity and pressure were holding steady. I knew that a thimble of oil spread by the airflow can give the appearance of a Texas "gusher", so the brown lines creeping back along the engine weren't particularly severe and failed to worsen over the ensuing hours. On a positive note, every valve, switch and tank of the ferry tanks operated seamlessly until finally Townsville loomed ahead in the windscreen.

It had been a long day, but there was still daylight left for the engineers to repair the jammed carburettor heat cable and assess the oil leak. As suspected, the left engine had just blown a little oil in the early stage of the flight and had arrived with a full and healthy supply at the end of eight hours in the air. Next, the ferry tanks were filled to the gunnels and the aircraft was put to bed for the night while Rick and I planned for the day ahead.

It was still dark when we arrived at the airport and met with the customs officials who vetted our passports and inspected our aeroplane. As we taxied out for takeoff, everything about the Islander felt heavy and sluggish as she did her best to cope with this very full load of fuel and two hardy souls. As we lined up on Runway 01, the beacon on top of Magnetic Island ahead blinked slowly and I wondered if the machine would be able to clear the island after takeoff. The answer was "no".

As the wheels left the ground, the Islander slowly took to the sky with effort but very little enthusiasm. All the while the red light blinked on and off. I eased the aircraft into a gentle left turn and gave the island a wide berth as we continued to slowly climb to our cruise altitude over the dark ocean below us. I looked down at my life jacket and the raft beside me, two very yellow reminders of the miles of water that lay ahead.

It seemed to take forever to get to 6,000 feet but we eventually did and trimmed out the aeroplane for level flight. She hummed along in harmony as I synchronised the spinning propellers and adjusted the fuel flow for the long leg ahead. Rick and I confirmed that all was in order with our plane and plan and then sat silently staring out into the black pre-dawn.

I handed control of the aeroplane to Rick and shone my torch on the floor between my legs where the ferry tank fuel selector panel was positioned. Reaching down I double-checked that I had a hold of the correct lever and then rotated it to redirect the fuel from the ferry tank at the rear. Having done so, I sat upright and logged the time and the fuel quantities remaining on a schematic that I had drawn up for the flight. I had just put my pencil back in my pocket when the left engine coughed....and then coughed again...and again.

I shone the torch back down on the fuel panel and grabbed the lever, ready to reselect the wing tanks. I felt an ever-so-slight *click* and the engine began to purr and my heart began to beat regularly once again. Evidently I had not quite pushed the lever fully to its limit which was a little beyond 90 degrees. Slowly my adrenalin levels returned to normal but I made a very large note to myself for all future fuel selections.

We were on our way again. In the darkness, the coastline of Australia slipped away behind us and all that lay ahead was darkness below and twinkling stars above. The first glimmer of daybreak had not yet crept above the horizon as I rubbed my eyes and contemplated the day ahead. When the engines next shut down I would be on a remote island and seemingly a world away from home.

***

14

Halfway to Paradise

With Townsville now out of sight and two more hours on the clock, the sun slowly rose and we shook off the shackles of night. The GPS pointed the way and we followed its lead towards Gurney Airport on the southern tip of New Guinea. Aside from a lone vessel, all that was to be seen was uninterrupted water in all directions. For two men in a small aeroplane, it was both daunting and picturesque. I had crossed this stretch of ocean previously; still, man was never designed to travel through the air beyond the sight of land. For millions of years clambering up a tree had been a significant achievement. I think we both appreciated the potential danger and untouched beauty that lay before us.

Slowly, that beautiful blue gave way to a jagged green edge on the horizon. New Guinea grew slowly closer and, bit by bit, features of the coastline could be distinguished, proving that the GPS had performed as promised. Occasional puffs of white cloud could be seen sitting on the ranges, but otherwise our path was clear as we passed over Gurney and set course for Manus Island.

Creeping along the back of New Guinea, navigation was made even easier as we checked off landmarks out to our left-hand side. I had flown in New Guinea a year earlier and tied a visual image to many of the towns that slid past on my chart. Inevitably my thoughts drifted to the jungles and the torrid fighting that had taken place during World War Two. I thought of my father who had died only months earlier and had seen action in those jungles as a mere teenager. I thought of my mother's fiancé who never came home and now lay in a grave to the country's north.

Rick and I spoke for periods on that long sector, but there were also long comfortable silences as we contemplated the world around us. When pilots share their passion of flight and the world below, it is as easily conveyed by silence as it is by words. There is the occasional pointing finger towards an atoll below or a knowing nod at the violent landscape surrounding a now-extinct volcano. Nothing much else needs to be said.

Soon the open waters of the Bismarck Sea beckoned as clouds began to gather in the afternoon heat. The isolated cumulus clouds began joining together to form a lower, greyer overcast and heavy showers of rain began to appear about us. We dialled up an old-style navigation beacon and tuned the frequency for Momote Airport on Manus Island. The needle sat lifeless on the instrument as we sat too low and beyond the signal's strength to receive any directional information. Still, the moving bar on the face of GPS sat in the middle of the dots telling us that we were "on track"...if we'd programmed the device correctly.

Eventually the needle came to life and wandered in a direction somewhere ahead of us. Now the cloud was solid overcast and the showers about us extremely thick as the fat tropical drops pelted down towards the waves below. We skipped left and right about the showers to avoid being trapped above the cloud layer and unable to descend into Momote.

Small islands began to appear with their isolated peaks, and the needle on the dial began to point dead ahead. The coast of Manus Island gradually emerged from the murk, but the airport was not immediately apparent. I made for land and hugged the coast, knowing that the runway could not be far away. Still, our tired eyes could not see it despite every navigation aid suggesting it was there.

Then, as we rounded a headland, the telltale gun-barrel jungle clearing which was the runway came into view. We reversed our turn and positioned off the coast to complete our checks and prepare the aircraft for its approach to land. By now the showers were closing in and rain occasionally thrashed at the windscreen as I lowered the flaps and descended towards the runway. It was with some relief that I slowly closed the throttles and allowed the Islander to settle on the runway, accompanied by a cacophony of clanging. It was an old World War Two airstrip, still covered in the pierced steel planking, or PSP, and the noise on touchdown was not insignificant.

After ten-and-a-half hours aloft, and the scratching of the high frequency radio in our ears, we finally gave the reliable little engines a rest as the propellers came to a halt.

We filled out our logs and then both swung our doors open to step out, draw a deep breath and stretch our legs. Almost immediately, villagers appeared from amongst the undergrowth and moved towards the drums of aviation fuel that were waiting for us.

We set about arranging the drums and hand-pump to fill our thirsty tanks to the brim for the next day's overwater flight to Yap Island. As we attended to the aeroplane, occasional visitors could be found opening doors and rummaging through the aircraft's lockers. Our requests to leave the aircraft alone were met with sidewards glances and muttered comments, still smiling with teeth stained scarlet from chewing Betel nut.

Manus Island had been home to a "cargo cult" in years past and now criminal Raskol gangs could be found amongst the population's number. There was an uneasy atmosphere as we checked the caps on the full fuel tanks and thanked the locals for their assistance. Some disappeared as fast as they had emerged and others stood at a distance, just looking at the Islander. I had been in New Guinea before, but had never felt this uncomfortable. Rick felt the same about the situation and we resolved to stay the night with the aircraft; in fact in the cockpit.

With the tanks filling the cabin, the only space left was in our seats. We ate a canned dinner and drank copious amounts of water before slowly the sun began to settle and the jungle's darkness crept over the airport. We climbed inside the Islander where the seats only rose uncomfortably half way up our backs. Stuffing jackets between the ferry tanks and our spines, we were able to nestle into a sort of half-foetal sleeping position.

The cockpit soon became hot and stale, so I slid the window open to give us some more ventilation and lessen the sweat running down my neck. I would no sooner begin to cool off than the relief would be replaced by the buzzing and occasional bite of insects. My mind raced to my father's tales of malaria during the war and I anticipated that I'd be shaking with the "cold sweats" any minute now. Occasionally a noise or a shuffle outside gained my attention, but a shine of the torch's beam silenced the sound without fail.

Somehow we both managed to get some REM sleep, only stirring again when the sun blared through the windscreen. Another stretch of the legs, some basic ablutions and we were both keen and ready to depart. The flight to Yap Island would be similar in time and distance as our first hop to Townsville, except these nine hours would be all over water.

We climbed away from Manus Island in the morning sunlight to fly a very remote passage aided by our compass, GPS and maps of little more than differing shades of blue. Having seen the GPS at work, I was very pleased to have it along for the ride and marvelled at its simple display relaying a wealth of information.

Hour after hour passed, with only small rocky outcrops and atolls to interrupt the endless ocean. I was amazed at how many of these isolated features had wrecked, rusting vessels rotting on their edges. One in particular resembled a funnel and the hapless crew had obviously sailed down its throat, only realising its terminal nature when it could no longer turn around. So many traps-in-waiting for ocean-going vessels, I thought, before re-checking our fuel, flight plan and the trusty GPS.

The Equator came and went and I counted down the minutes of latitude until they became seconds and finally the GPS display flicked from South to North. What a wonder this technology is; an innocent little grey box that looks towards the heavens and calculates its position using the man-made satellites hurtling across the heavens. Man is so clever; we can span oceans in tiny craft and know exactly where we are to the exact inch.

Not long after I had this thought the GPS went entirely blank.

It seems that the GPS's heritage was military in origin and at any particular time access to the navigational data could be switched off for the common man. Unfortunately, this common man was now looking at a magnetic compass bobbling in a glass sphere of alcohol and endless miles of ocean.

Rick and I exchanged glances and, given his missionary vocation, I refrained from verbalising the word that first leapt into my head when the GPS failed. Our first thought was of our fuel. Fundamentally, fuel equals time and time equals options. We had departed Manus Island with around 16 hours of fuel on board, so we had a few options. We could effectively fly to where we calculated that Yap should be and still have enough fuel to turn left and fly to the Philippines. Heck, we could nearly make Taiwan. So we had time.

Honing down our alternatives, we assessed that we were flying towards Micronesia and there were more islands than simply Yap alone. Many of these islands had beacons that we could home in on regardless of the GPS, just as we had done at Manus. Finally, the ocean ahead was Rick's backyard. His job with the organisation saw him island-hopping this region every day. Except for isolated clean white cumulus clouds, the weather was brilliant. We decided to hold our course and fly "old school" towards Micronesia and refine our navigation as we began to accumulate features.

Charts, pencils and compass at the ready, we steered the Islander onward. Then, as quickly as it had blanked, it blinked, and the GPS returned. However, it had betrayed my trust once without warning so I warily watched it, still with map in hand. After eight hours of flight that had seesawed between bliss and bewilderment, an island rose from the ocean ahead, right on time. It was Yap.

Thirteen miles long and in the middle of nowhere, this lush green oasis was surrounded by crystal clear shallows and reefs of brilliant colours. And yet it sat just to the south of the considerable depths of the Marianas Trench. Its beauty was idyllic and all-consuming as I flew the Islander around the circuit and brought her back to earth after nearly three days, 30 hours of flight and 3,000 miles. Rick was home and part of me felt that I was too.

The welcome was of the warmest kind, as the community looked upon its newest island life-line with its red and white paint. Conversation was at an electric pace and handshakes were firm and frequent. I was now looking forward to a few days enjoying the sights of this island paradise and its people without the sound of the Islander's engines droning in my ears. I had safely reached my destination, but I was soon to learn that this journey was far from over.

***

15

BEYOND PARADISE

My time on the small Micronesian island was magical. The waters of Yap were as blue as I had ever seen and every beach was like a postcard setting. It was such a small island that it had managed to remain relatively untouched by the ever-advancing world around it. Walking paths weaved through the lush jungle and giant stone discs that represented a form of currency sat outside traditional wooden halls. The people were amongst the most welcoming that I had ever met, possessing a humble generosity we could all learn from.

Its peaceful nature belied the fact that it had been in the midst of the horror of World War Two. It had been occupied by the Japanese and then liberated by the advancing allied forces as they island-hopped their way to Tokyo. It had been heavily bombed by the allies in 1944 as the airstrip at Yap still hosts a number of Japanese aircraft. Evidence of the conflict remains with naval vessels rusting offshore and the barrels of old anti-aircraft guns jutting out from the ground cover. There were even murmurs that the wrecks of old aircraft were to be found in the surrounding waters and these particularly heightened my interest.

By all accounts, the wrecks were a diver's paradise, with natural beauty and the remnants of war both alive beneath the surface. I befriended a local lad and came to discuss the aircraft wreckages that might remain. At first he cited the skeleton of a Boeing 727 that had crashed a decade before, but soon he gathered that I meant the aircraft from the war. He nodded knowingly and agreed to take me to see the site of the old Japanese airfield.

With Rick we rode in the back of the utility truck over bumpy tracks lined by lush green foliage. Quite suddenly, we emerged into a clearing; a long straight clearing. It was unmistakably a runway and I could already see one wreck in amongst the bush. The truck came to a halt and we wandered over to the tall tail section of a Japanese bomber. Only a short distance away lay the cockpit and it was if the aircraft had been broken in two at some point, perhaps during a bombing raid. I scrambled amongst the twisted metal and my imagination started to picture the world that this bomber had seen. I paused for a moment and could almost see the young Japanese faces, their helmets and goggles. Where was it that this crew finally called home?

Those images became increasingly vivid after I walked from the bomber and came upon a number of Japanese Zero fighters. They were in varying stages of disrepair, but one was still sitting on its landing gear. The wings and flanks were peppered with bullet holes where they had been ruthlessly strafed where they stood. I ran my fingers around the edges of these holes and surveyed the shattered fighter, struggling to stand after nearly half a century.

Like the bomber, the fighters were covered in a clay-red coating that had served to protest the airframe against corrosion; a task it had performed admirably. Bare firewalls showed the ends of metal fittings and brackets where the engine had once been fixed, but still the cockpits remained. I climbed inside and squatted where the pilot had once sat, looking at a panel full of round holes where instruments had once been situated. There was an absence of heavy armour-plating around the cockpit that was standard on allied fighters and I thought of what this meant both in terms of manoeuvrability and mortality.

The control stick still remained and I moved it from side to side in the way it had once moved in combat in the skies above. My young friend rested on the cockpit's edge as I pointed to the missing instruments wistfully. He related that they had all been there until recent times, but a Japanese group had taken them when they visited the island to take possession of a number of other Zeros. My ears pricked up at the mention of even more aircraft and my interest did not go unnoticed. He leaned over and quietly whispered, "There is another".

We rejoined his father and Rick and set off in the truck once more. This time when we came to a halt, there was no clearing just green foliage. We edged our way down the slope and the long grass developed into thick undergrowth. With vines twisting all around, a canopy of sorts formed overhead through which the sun broke in shards of light. The air was stagnant in this cocoon and the sweat rolled down my face and back. And then I saw it.

At first it was a lone undercarriage leg pointing skyward, its tyre long perished. I could see immediately that the aircraft was inverted but it was not until I drew closer that I discovered the true intrigue. I could now determine that the paint colour was dark blue and I sensed that this was not a Japanese aircraft but a United States Navy fighter. Now, standing beside the crippled fighter, I could make out that it was a Hellcat and, considering its situation, aside from numerous large calibre holes, it was incredibly intact.

Strangely, its landing gear and flaps were both extended. I wondered if the pilot had tried to land on the jungle canopy, or simply slow the aircraft to its minimum speed before impact. So many questions ran through my mind and I could not help but wonder about the fate of the pilot. I asked my friends and the elder replied that he was killed and buried by the local inhabitants, motioning up the slope as he spoke.

My heart sank a little as the condition of the aeroplane suggested that he just might have survived. Again, in my mind I placed myself in the cockpit of the stricken Hellcat and wondered how I would have coped in the brutal skies of war. Most likely the pilot was younger than me, a mere boy of around 20 years of age or so. He would have played sport and made model aircraft in his school years, but who could have seen that his life would have ended inverted, in a jungle on a small island in the middle of the Pacific.

I lingered by the Hellcat's remains until the time came to return to my lodgings. Despite the wonderful times I had during my remaining days on Yap, I could not shake the faceless image of a young pilot and his wrecked fighter. It moved me deeply and filled my thoughts as I lay awake at night waiting for sleep to visit me.

My stay on Yap had shown me so much in so little time; from the wonderful people and captivating scenery to the history and the horror that echoed from the war's remains. As I packed my bag to fly out on the airliner the next day, the conversation in the next room became increasingly rapid. It transpired that a medical evacuation was to take place to transport a gentleman to Guam, about 500 miles away over water.

The conundrum was that, even though the gentleman was in a stable condition, a medico would be required to escort him to manage his intravenous line. In turn, his absence would significantly reduce the island's own medical coverage. Having been a paramedic in times past, I offered to monitor the IV line if that was of any assistance; I was due to fly out to Guam in the morning anyway. A short time later I was airborne in the cabin of a Beechcraft Queen Air, having bid the good people of Yap Island farewell.

Unfortunately, when we arrived in Guam the authorities were prepared to accept the patient, but not the unannounced passenger.

My documentation stated that my arrival in Guam was for the following day and I could not enter before that, no exceptions. The missionary pilot pleaded my case but it was to no avail. I could return to Yap and fly back the next morning or I could spend the night in a holding facility as a guest of the government authorities.

The second option came with too many question marks, so I boarded the Queen Air once again and we flew the 500 miles back to Yap in darkness. My arrival allowed me enough time to shower, shave and bid farewell to my new friends one more time before I boarded the airliner for Guam and, ultimately, Australia.

It had only been a matter of 10 days from departing Sydney to ferry the Islander to Yap until the airliner buried the landing back on Australian soil, springing open the overhead lockers and dropping the oxygen masks. Yet in that short window of time I had seen and experienced so much.

I have travelled a good many more miles in the years since Yap, but a pilot's experience is more than the miles behind and the hours logged. It is the people and the places and the ability to interact as a friend rather than a hotel guest. Like so many of my experiences before my airline career began, I slept and ate in people's homes and visited places far off the beaten track. I was cast beyond my comfort zone time and again.

The greatest memories grew from spontaneous actions and twists of fate to embed themselves in my very fibre. Flight has taken me to places that I never would have seen, where I've felt the warmth of people that I never would have met. And even those I never met, those young faceless pilots in the jungle, they too have become a part of me. Even today, I salute their bravery and recall their tragic end. Separated by generations and nautical miles, for me their sacrifice will never be forgotten.

***

A Japanese 'Zero' on Yap Island.

The poignant remains of the 'Hellcat' on Yap Island.

16

JUST A COUNTRY AIRFIELD

It is always worth advancing with one eye cast over one's shoulder.

Whether conducting a flight on a sunny day and checking whether those clouds are closing in behind, or forging a new frontier and choosing to respect the lessons of the past.

Hindsight is not merely 20/20 vision, it is a building block provided by those that have gone before.

These building blocks can take many forms; from air crash investigations to a wise old pilot's words of warning in the "back bar". Regardless of the means of delivery, credible, respected knowledge is worth its weight in gold, and yet it is so often provided free of charge to those who possess the patience to pause, look and listen.

Recently, I walked away from the computer keyboard, files and manuals that are the life-blood of my writing. With my family, we drove along rolling ridges and through sun-struck Canola fields until we came upon a small country township. At first glance, it offered the usual sights of a rural setting: livestock, harvesters and main streets that are wide enough to turn a bullock team. But drive a little through the town and there's more – very much more.

A few kilometres out of town and over the railway line lay Temora Airport. In the dark days of World War Two, this airfield was the thriving home to No.10 Elementary Flying Training School (EFTS). It was here that many of the Empire's pilots of that conflict first took to the sky and earned their wings in the timeless deHavilland Tiger Moth. It was a training scheme that spanned the Commonwealth, from Canada to South Africa.

As you wander about the airfield, some original barracks and buildings still remain, while more modern memorials provide a tribute to those who have gone before. It is a scene repeated at various corners of the globe at small country airfields. Almost forgotten today, they were once pivotal facilities in a world at war. And should you opt to explore a little further, you'll undoubtedly discover some old foundations or a patch of hardstand concealed amongst the grass. Yet, in this digital age, this country town still has something very special to offer and some lessons from yesteryear still to heed; for it is home to a very special aviation museum.

It is special because it is a living, breathing museum. The aircraft still fly and the words of veterans are there for all to see upon its walls and through its oral histories. However, it is on the flying days that some real magic happens. Those wondrous aeroplanes that flew in support of the Commonwealth's freedom across the years come to life and fill the skies with sounds and sights that are now so rarely witnessed. Between the dashing flypast of a Spitfire, or the gentle roll of a Gloster Meteor, the words of veterans are there to be heard. Their voices have weakened ever so slightly with the passage of time, but their memories are still crystal clear as they are released once again through the loudspeakers overhead. Men and women who served selflessly in a very different time share their insights with the gathered crowd. The modern-day pilots of these vintage machines offer their expert insights, and then it's time for another graceful sweep of the sky by another graceful set of wings.

Back at sea level there are active workshops to view from the gallery, other veteran aircraft to admire and walls and walls of photographs and tales. Many of the specific skills required to keep these aircraft aloft are passed down from engineer to engineer; no longer taught in technical colleges or your regular hangar. It is a pleasure to watch true tradesman at work, preserving and conserving, while the world outside is one of "new and improved" models and a throwaway mindset.

Then the sound of a Merlin engine catches the ear and all heads tilt skyward, shielding the sun in an informal salute. While modern aviation is dominated by fuel-efficient twin turbo-fans, the air show gives the sky personality; a face and a heartbeat. Graceful silhouettes and magical sounds intermingle with the occasional cloud and the lightest of breezes. And yet, even these majestic aircraft are merely inert metal without the people behind them. From those veterans of yesteryear to the professionals of today, it is the people and their passion that breathe life into these wonderful machines.

And when the display has finished and the Merlin's sigh is replaced by the chug of the tractor putting the aircraft to bed, there are still special moments to be found. As the sun sits lower and the breeze flicks the top of the blades of the long grass, a few keen airmen seek to grab the last rays of light and skip through the sky one last time. Seated silently where those pioneers once walked, an aerobatic Pitts stall-turns overhead and an RV10 closes the throttle as the "piano keys" pass beneath. They are new sounds being sung by new aircraft in a new world, saluting the roar of those aircraft that have gone before.

Aircraft and airmen are always well advised to build upon those lessons already learned. The nostalgia of air shows can bring those lessons alive through both men and machines of a bygone time and all the grace that comes with them. And then, once the excitement has passed and the day is nearly done, find a quiet corner and sit down amongst the grass. If you listen ever so carefully you might hear the wind passing through the wires of a biplane, or catch a whisper from those excited youths who were valiant airmen in darker days. Sit back, forget the world as it is and take in what it once was. At a humble country airfield, such a dream is still within your reach.

***

17

A Balancing Act

My D55 Baron looked a little worse for wear, but I couldn't have been happier. When I say "worse for wear", she was decidedly untidy on the outside with about 40% of her airframe painted in green primer and the remainder in her faded factory scheme. In fact, one day on the apron at a regional airport, a Fokker F50 crew taxied past, mouths agape, at the sight of my little machine. In fairness, you must remember that this was a freight workhorse and not a show pony.

At her heart this was a fantastic little aeroplane. Even after many years of service, the airframe was dead straight and trimmed out beautifully. The D55 Baron also had the upgraded 285HP engine, which gave it a little extra "zip factor", and when blended with Beechcraft's wonderful control feel, was an absolute joy to fly. There were still the idiosyncrasies of the Beech's single "throw-over" control wheel and reversed throttle and pitch levers, but nothing that impeded the task at hand.

Known as "bank running", which involves flying out from a regional centre, I had taken off from Wagga Wagga, around first light and delivered freight to multiple ports before parking the aircraft for the day at around 9:30am. The rest of the day would be spent in limbo in a country hotel room, alternating between naps and daytime television; the latter usually inducing further naps. That afternoon I would return to the aircraft and retrace the morning's route in reverse order, gathering freight along the way. On reaching my base once again, along with other Barons, I would divest my payload to a waiting Mitsubishi MU-2 which would make a beeline to the state's capital, Sydney.

The afternoon's sense of urgency was exacerbated by the nature of the freight. It comprised of critical bank documents that were required in the city counting rooms before the close of business. Occasionally there were also highly guarded bags of cash that rode up front on the passenger seat and had to be personally handed over at the sector's end. As all of the "bank bags" were neither heavy nor large in size, the freight operator sold off the additional space for anything else requiring rapid transport at a premium price. This included Express Post mail, courier satchels and just about anything else you can imagine. However, nothing was to delay the bank bags.

Friday afternoons were always a little different. The banks closed later, as did the counting rooms in Sydney. The road couriers who delivered the freight to the aeroplane always seemed to have an extra degree of speed and purpose. It was possibly a combination of the bank's final day of takings combined with a genuine urge to be rid of me and on their way to an end-of-week ale.

Whatever the reason, speed was of the essence one particular Friday. I had just made my third and final pick-up and was about to depart to rendezvous with the MU-2 when my pager started buzzing on my hip. These were the days when the very rare mobile phone was about the size and shape of a house brick. The instructions were to bypass my home port of Wagga, make three other pick-ups and then head directly to Sydney. This was great news as my girlfriend, now wife, lived in Sydney.

I departed for the first additional port of call and ran some numbers en route. Fuel was not a problem as I always filled the tanks at the end of the run each morning, allowing the burn-off in the afternoon to open up freight capacity for the next day. With three pick-ups, weight was rarely a factor, but now with six I would have to keep my eye closely on the growing payload. Fortunately, I had devised a master "weight and balance" sheet that I used each day, religiously ticking off the weight and position of my load at each port of call before filing the freight manifest. The situation was well in hand and I looked forward to the variety of some different airfields and the challenge of making it to Sydney before the counting rooms closed.

While the '55 series Baron was a great little aeroplane, there were a couple of areas where she could fall short as a freight carrier. Firstly, the D55 had a small luggage door on the starboard side that was used to load freight on the "hot" turnarounds with one engine running. Without the large double doors of the later B58, the couriers would do their best to crawl in and load the freight behind my seat and cargo net.

I always encouraged the loaders to load the '55 as far forward as possible, particularly when it came to heavy items. On my regular route I had built up a good rapport with the ground staff and explained why this was a preferable method of loading. The issue was that the '55 Baron could quite easily go out the aft limits of its "centre of gravity" if care wasn't taken. Furthermore, as fuel was burnt from the main tanks, the "centre of gravity" crept even further aft. This balance issue was the other shortcoming of the '55 Baron in the freight world.

Only a year before, a chap I knew died when his B55 Baron crashed at night with a full load of passengers and ski equipment on board. The ATSB report had stated that from ATC radar displays, "The aircraft exhibited flight characteristics consistent with those of an aircraft loaded to an aft centre of gravity position. There are indications that the centre of gravity moved further aft during the flight, until reaching a point at which the pilot was unable to prevent significant diversions in both climb and descent from the reference altitude, culminating in the rapid descent."

For the fortunately uninitiated, with an aft CofG, the aircraft becomes inherently unstable in the "pitching plane". When pulling back on the stick, the aircraft wants to continue pitching upwards until positive forward force is exerted, and then it wants to continue pitching down. The pilot who died that night was confronted with an ever-increasing cycle of climbs and descents of increasing intensity which was plotted at over 4,000 fpm on the final, fatal descent. Understandably, I was quite particular about the loading of my Baron.

Aware of my aeroplane's shortcomings and well prepared, I set course for my final pick-up. I had progressively added my freight manifests and calculated that I could take no more than 20kg before departing for Sydney. As such, I could only safely lift the bank bags and Express Post envelopes, and made a note to that effect on my paperwork.

As I pulled up on the apron, I shut one engine down and the courier poked his head through the cargo door, yelling, "How much can you take?" I replied with my figure of 20kg and added that the bank bags were about my limit. He withdrew through the hatch and, I heard the bags thrown on board and the hatch shut. The courier then climbed on the wing and handed me my manifest through the door. It was made out for exactly 20kg. I should have been suspicious at that point, but in the hurried world of bank running, I wasn't.

Without further ado, the courier hopped off the wing and I started the shut-down engine. With both turning, I taxied away and completed my pre take-off sequences before entering and backtracking down the main runway. Turning around on the piano keys, I could feel that the aircraft was heavier than usual, although there was nothing dramatic to note. I advanced the throttles and accelerated, noting my critical speeds as I prepared to rotate.

As I was about to pull back on the control column, the nose started to unstick of its own will. I checked the rotation with a touch of forward pressure and set the attitude for the climb. I knew immediately that the aircraft was out the back end of the CofG envelope, so I gingerly nursed my little Baron aloft. In this situation, the controls feel so light that it's as if you don't have control, and it is decidedly unsettling.

As the nosewheel retracted to the rear, I decided to hold off for the moment until I had some space between the earth and my aeroplane. To retract the gear would have brought the weight of the nosewheel aft and I wanted that mass hanging as far forward on the moment arm as I could get it. Slowly the Baron climbed away as I maintained runway heading, not risking the tilted lift vector of a turn. As the altitude accumulated to around 800 feet, I could still feel the aircraft teetering gingerly on the edge and she wasn't exactly setting the world on fire with climb performance. I switched one side to the auxiliary fuel tank as, unlike the main tanks, this will burn the CofG forward. When this engine was definitely running steadily from the "aux", I selected the auxiliary tank on the other side. Relatively quickly, I started to feel an improvement in the handling characteristics.

Now at a safe height, but still on runway heading, I retracted the gear and felt a twinge in the aircraft's balance as I retrimmed the aircraft for the cruise climb. Minute after minute passed and the aircraft became more and more manageable to fly as the balance righted itself. However, the climb performance continued to be far less than spectacular until I finally levelled off. The run home was now not that much further than returning to the departure field and the aircraft was starting to behave normally, so I set course for Sydney. Furthermore, I wanted to burn the auxiliary tanks "forward" as far as possible before selecting the main tanks once again for landing.

I seethed on that final sector, well aware of how I had been duped. The courier was going to write 20kg on that manifest whatever he decided to load on board, unaware of the severe consequences it could have on the flight stability of the aeroplane. My statement to him should have been simply that I could only take the bank bags, full stop. Even so, with the obscured view of the cargo hatch, he could've sneaked in a printing press for all I could observe.

My arrival was without event and as I climbed from the Baron, a handful of ground staff congratulated me on a great job in getting the extra load to Sydney on time. I launched into a mentally rehearsed vitriol of how that load had almost cost me my neck and demanded that the load be weighed. They were not quite so happy about the delay that would incur, but they were very aware that I was very serious about this breach.

It was decades ago now and my recollection of the final number escapes me, but suffice it to say that final uplift was in excess of 20kg. I was not only overloaded, but, critically, I was overloaded to the rear, forcing the aircraft's CofG out of the aft limit of the envelope. It was not a massive overload, but it was enough to have the aircraft's controllability teetering on the brink and me sweating on the outcome.

I could not help but think how helpless my old mate must have felt that dark night over the hills as his Baron began to describe ever increasing arcs. I wondered if he'd realised what was happening when the autopilot seemingly let loose under the burden of imbalance. Could he have yelled at his passengers to clamber forward over the seats to shift the CofG? They are all moot points now as the investigation report will attest.

Personally, that afternoon reinforced the importance of knowing your aircraft's limitations and flying well within them. In retrospect, with such a critical final uplift, I should have dispensed with the hot turnaround, shut the aircraft down and supervised the loading. Like James Reason's "Swiss Cheese" model, the danger arose from a series of events rather than a sole instigating factor. I was the "final filter" and let it slip through by staying in my seat as the aft-most payload was put aboard. Mind you, it would be ideal to be able to trust the figures represented on the manifest too.

It was one such incident in what has been, to date, a fascinating career. As pilots, it is best to always review and learn from such incidents to avoid falling into the same trap again. Sometimes that trap may be the force of Mother Nature and on other occasions it may stem from the aircraft itself. On that Friday afternoon, the trap was set by a few wayward boxes and an incorrect manifest. Ultimately, they combined to present me with a very challenging balancing act.

***

18

A Different Approach

I was a flight instructor nudging 30 and flying was my life. My worldly belongings fitted comfortably into the boot of a car, making it easy for me to fly anywhere at a moment's notice. However, my passion exacted its price: How was I going to find someone with whom to settle down if I was always taking wing?

I was reflecting on this very situation late one afternoon as the winter sun started to move towards the horizon behind me. At 5,500 feet, the cockpit of our single-engine Aerospatiale Trinidad had started to absorb the winter chill outside, though my student was sweating as he checked charts and flight logs in a flurry of pencils and paper. With his head down, he missed the first flicker of the plane's digital read-out. There was a potential problem with the flow of fuel, I noticed, and then the gauge flickered ominously again.

As we cruised over the hills of the Great Dividing Range, jutting 3,500 feet above sea level, the engine continued to run steady, though my eye was already starting to hunt for a place to land…just in case. There was rugged terrain all around us, but a small clearing lay right below us. It wasn't big enough, but any patch devoid of towering trees was encouraging.

The gauge flickered again, and this time the engine surged and coughed. It paused, then roared and coughed again. My student actuated switches and valves as per the checklist, all to no avail. I took over the controls and advised Sydney Flight Service of our predicament. Our plane's pause periods now outweighed its surges of power and we were struggling to maintain height. Then the engine failed completely and our aeroplane became a glider.

I broadcast a Mayday call and briefed my student to secure loose items in the cockpit and evacuate without delay once we were down. As I wheeled around in a descending left hand turn, the world loomed very large in the window and the landing field looked incredibly short. I could suddenly hear my late-father's voice when he was teaching me to fly: "Fly the aeroplane… and fly your airspeed!" I'm sure he was in the aeroplane with me that day.

Feeling confident we would reach the field, I lowered the landing gear and flaps and switched off the electrics to minimise the chance of post-impact fire. As I aligned the aircraft with the field I decided it was way too short to make it over the trees and still pull up at the far end. So, as I had done on airstrips in the outback and New Guinea, I slipped the aircraft down between the trees. Foliage rushed by us and then the wheels hit. Thump!

Eighty miles an hour across an unprepared surface is a wild ride. I was on the brakes and hoping for the best when a sizeable rock jutted up ahead. Unable to swerve to any great degree, I tensed my guts and for a nanosecond imagined the control wheel spearing into me. Bang! The right landing gear struck the rock, but we were okay; hurtling across the paddock, but okay. With not enough room for my liking, I heaved back on the wheel and kicked in my right boot, slewing the aircraft to a halt. I swung around to tell my student to get out and found myself staring at an open cockpit door and a human form sprinting away. He sure knew how to follow instructions!

The lights of Sydney have rarely looked as welcoming as they did that night as our rescue helicopter took us to hospital. Adrenalin was still coursing through my veins and I began to reflect for the first time on how close I had come to not making it home. In that moment, I started to question some of my priorities. Perhaps I should pay attention to other aspects of my life because they just might not be there tomorrow? As this thought struck me, the vision of a young female instructor with whom I worked popped up in my mind's eye. I'd always thought of her as young and fun, and assumed there was no future there because I was older and more serious. But as the rotors whirred above the hospital's helipad, I wasn't so sure anymore.

A cursory hospital check and discharge later, I made my way back to the airport and the Royal Aero Club bar. And whose was the first face I was to see? My female flight instructor friend looked genuinely happy to see me, expressing relief that I had not made the headlines on the evening news. We proceeded to chat late into the night. Perhaps it was the adrenalin, or the celebratory drinks being served at the Aero Club, but I relaxed and began to open up. I wasn't baring my soul - that would have been too great a deviation - but I cracked open the door a bit.

As it turned out, that long day and night was a point of no return. And the outcome? This year that "young, fun flight instructor" and I celebrated our 17th wedding anniversary in the company of our four children: Ruby, Hannah, Elizabeth and Hayden. True love strikes in mysterious ways, they say, but who would have thought it would take an engine failure to make a reluctant bachelor change his ways?

***

19

Silence Aloft

This was a wedding anniversary present where everyone wins. The plan was for a hot-air balloon ride followed by a gourmet breakfast amongst the lawns and sandstone pillars of our state's original Government House. All that was needed was to arrive on time, well before dawn, and dress to keep the biting frost at bay. Kirrily and I couldn't wait.

The frosty lawns of Government House crunched beneath our feet and patches of fog lurked ominously, illuminated by the old-world lamp-posts that lined the entrance while a full moon shone down from a clear sky. Dawn was not far away as our pilot gathered the group of eight together to outline the day's events. The first challenge was to determine if there was any wind, as this would allow us to plan our launch site so that we would drift back on the breeze in time for that hot breakfast.

The pilot held a small, helium-filled balloon with a disposable coffee cup tethered beneath in one hand. He tipped the cup over towards a lit match to light a candle fixed inside. The wick grabbed hungrily at the flame. With that the balloon was freed and it began to drift slowly upwards; at first straight up and then slowly to the north. All the while the pilot timed its progress second by second, mentally calculating at what height the favourable winds were to be found. The balloon continued to float up into the northern sky until the glowing cup was lost amidst the twinkling morning stars.

The plan was now in place. We were bundled into a big four-wheel-drive vehicle with a large trailer, weighed down by a sizeable wicker basket, or "gondola", and all manner of apparatus. The sun was beginning to rise when we arrived at a vacant football field. Quickly the vast balloon was laid out with its scarlet and canary stripes looking like a massive lollipop against the frost. It was then secured to the gondola which was topped with a large metallic "burner" that would generate the trapped parcel of hot air that would lift us.

When all was in order, the pilot brought the rig to life by a small fan, half-inflating the vast balloon with cold ambient air before the burner was ignited and the first breaths a hot air poured in. Slowly the balloon began to gently bob about, battling to lift its weight against gravity's hand. A little more air and a little more lift and it rose just a fraction further from the ground. After about 30 minutes, it hung lazily above the gondola and our group was guided over the sides of the basket to stand at the ready for flight.

Holding onto the sides, the pilot converted the gentle puffs of air into a constant roar from the burner. The balloon went taut, puffing out its chest, while the cables above the gondola surrendered any remaining slack. Then, without racing down a runway at pace, and without thumping rotors above our heads, we left the ground. Straight up like an elevator as the frost fell away and we looked down on the trees and goalposts.

This was not flight as I knew it. At this altitude of a few hundred feet, the world should be rushing by as a blur and my eyes should be hunting ahead for obstacles and errant birds. But this was a completely different type of flying. The pilot was now content with the altitude and the burner had fallen silent, allowing us to drift upon the breeze. Yet there was no chill on our faces as we were as one with the wind, buoyed like a bottle on the tide. We had no rudder and our course was at the mercy of the gods, who decided where to push us in this parcel of air.

Below, the world still slept, oblivious to our presence as we wafted above their roofs, lawns and swing-sets. Only their dogs seemed to sense the drifting humans overhead, barking at the sky and breaking the silence. We spoke quietly, as it seemed that every word would be free to fall from the gondola and disturb our surroundings. At times the balloon was still, holding station over one rooftop waiting for our driving force to blow gently once again. When our balloon began to drift a little lower, the burner would erupt for a short burst and the earth would drop away again, just a little. Each time the flame leapt to life, its glow warmed our cheeks and crept comfortably down our collars. This must be as close to a magic carpet ride as one can get.

Inside, the cockpit was as simple as the theory behind the balloon's powers of flight. A wicker basket with a couple of gauges, a valve and a good deal of judgement appeared to be the only tools at the pilot's disposal. Above us, the yellow-and-red-striped balloon extended a further hundred feet into the sky, embracing more than 200,000 cubic feet of warmed air. Between bursts from the burner, the pilot would point out landmarks and indicate where he hoped the wind would take us. The city skyline was silhouetted by the rising sun, which only added to the wonder of the flight.

We tracked across the suburbs one by one as our pace began to subtly increase. The houses were not a blur, but we were no longer lightly stepping from roof to roof either. The pilot scratched at his beard and eyed the way ahead. He mentioned that the wind had now picked up, however the direction was constant and we were tracking straight for our planned landing fields. Still, he doubted that our landing would now be a slow, vertical descent to kiss the grass and thought that we may well have forward motion.

As I was beginning to consider the ramifications of his assessment, he began to brief us where to sit in the gondola for landing and where to hold on; just in case. My wife and I weren't particularly fazed, as it all seemed like a sensible precaution, however there were a few worried faces beginning to show amongst the group.

We were all ready for the landing when the open parklands near Old Government House came into view. At first it was the tall lush trees that we sighted, but the large rolling green fields were close behind and looked far friendlier. Our rate of closure was much quicker than our dawdling pace at the flight's beginning, but it was nothing extreme. The pilot had allowed the air to cool and lower our trajectory towards the fields. There was another burst of hot air to ensure that we cleared the tops of the trees that were now close enough for us to see their individual leaves.

On the pilot's word, we all sat down and waited for the landing. There were no more bursts of air and no sound of rushing breeze as we braced silently on the gondola's floor. Waiting, waiting, waiting. It all seemed to be very calm and gentle and I pondered the colourful balloon overhead that was now set to the backdrop of a brilliant blue sky. The first indication that the landing was imminent was when the graunching sound of grass on wicker came through the basket's floor. It grew a little louder and a little bumpier but I could sense that we were almost at a standstill. And then the gondola tipped on its side. My wife and I laughed as it was an exciting conclusion to the flight, although the pilot seemed a little embarrassed. I felt some empathy, as I suspect it was similar to getting an airliner safely near the runway in a howling crosswind, only to have the final few feet result in a thump that makes the passengers gasp.

We righted ourselves and were guided to our waiting vehicle by the balloon's support crew that had delivered us to the football field an hour earlier. Soon we were seated on the historic verandah with white linen tablecloths and glasses of chilled champagne. The conversation was excited and I couldn't help but think that our less-than-graceful landing had actually added to the experience for everyone.

For me, the flight had been captivating. I marvelled at the skill, simplicity and silence of it and I enjoyed the thought that this was the means by which man had first ascended into the skies 200 years ago – and it still retained a regalness that its original pilots must have felt. This was not about man's machinery overpowering the laws of nature; it was about man politely hitching a ride. Perhaps the real majesty hung on those still moments, free of the burner and the barking dogs and hanging motionless in space with no apparent force or effort. The absolute peace of the silence aloft.

***

20

So Close…A Wartime Tragedy.

Francis "Frank" Owen Smith hailed from the peaceful, rural environs of New South Wales in Australia. By contrast, on March 13th 1945 he found himself serving with the Royal Australian Air Force on a bombing mission over the dark, chaotic jungle of New Guinea's north. Serving as the Wireless Air Gunner (WAG) on a 100 Squadron DAP Bristol Beaufort, it was his crew's 85th bombing sortie and their return to Australia was only weeks away.

Under the steady hand of the highly competent F/Lt Jack Fowler, Beaufort A9-650 lined up on the Japanese occupied village of Milak. It was just as they had trained and executed together so many times before. Target steady. Bomb release. The following Australian Beaufort reported seeing an explosion that engulfed '650 in flames. Disintegrating as it fell to earth; the bomber impacted the earth at high speed. There was to be no homecoming.

Born in 1922, Frank Smith hailed from inland township of Manilla in country New South Wales, before his family relocated to the dairy region of Kempsey on the northern coast of the same state. Originally working in the local retail stores, Frank had a passion for photography, though World War II meant that all such ambitions were to be placed on hold.

He was accepted by the RAAF in September 1941 for aircrew. At only 5'3", he barely made the height requirement. Initially held on reserve, he commenced training in April 1942 and was selected for training in the role of Wireless Air Gunner. He completed training in February 1943 and was commissioned in the rank of Pilot Officer. He was subsequently posted to an Operational Training Unit (OTU), where he would become familiar with his new aircraft, the DAP Bristol Beaufort.

It was during this training that he first met with the core of his crew, from which that unique friendship of airmen would grow. The captain was P/O H.J. "Jack" Fowler and the fellow WAG was P/O Jack Shipman, with whom Frank had already undertaken training.

From their operational conversion, they moved to the opposite side of the broad Australian continent to Western Australia where they joined 14 Squadron in mid-1943. Based out of Pearce, they would spend over a year honing their operational skills. During this time, on January 6th 1944, they would tragically lose their commanding officer, Wing Commander Charles Learmonth, DFC and bar, who had been decorated during the Battle of the Bismarck Sea. His Beaufort (A9-346) crashed into the sea off the Western Australian coast and was one of a number of DAP Beauforts lost under a cloud of mystery in this period. As Learmonth's fatal training flight unraveled, he was able to relay problems relating to his aircraft's controllability which ultimately lead to the lethal problem with the Beaufort's elevator.

Frank was well regarded by those around him and his senior officers. His assessment reports reflect a well liked young man "who possessed considerable ability considering his youth and inexperience". He and Jack Shipman in particular had developed a close friendship as the two WAGs had been with each other for most of their RAAF experience. Now they were on the cusp of disembarking together and seeing active service.

Frank had recently been promoted to Flying Officer and in August 1944, along with Fowler and Shipman he was posted to 100 Squadron RAAF based out of Tadji, New Guinea. Here they teamed up with a new navigator, P/O Geoff Waite M.I.D, who had already seen active service on Hudsons. Jack Fowler had earned a sound reputation as a commander throughout his training and subsequent postings. Under his leadership, Frank and the rest of the crew melded into an efficient unit.

100 Squadron bombing operations of this period centred on the Aitape-Wewak region and were flown in support of the Australian ground troops of the 6th Division. The RAAF and Australian Army worked in close co-operation, with Army observers flying aboard the Beauforts on occasions. Many times, the ground troops marked and called bombing runs on targets only a couple of hundred yards from their own position. The Beauforts often provided "default artillery" support that was not available to ground forces and the "diggers" who benefited were quick to recognise the significance of 100 Squadron's contribution in their battle of the Japanese XVIII Army.

On the morning of January 20th 1945, Frank Smith was lucky to escape when his Beaufort crashed on landing at Tadji. The aircraft was A9-557 and the crew had flown over half of their 60-odd missions to date in this aircraft. Along with an observing Army Captain Nancarrow, they had attacked a target at Elimi village received a sizeable amount of ground fire in the process. Complicating matters further, one of their 40 lb 'frag' bombs failed to release properly and was now 'live' and lying in the bomb bay.

Unable to dislodge the bomb by any means, Fowler opted for a flapless landing in an effort to make the touchdown as smooth as possible. This he achieved satisfactorily as the wheels rolled onto the Tadji runway, but on applying the brakes only a slight deceleration resulted before the brakes totally failed. As the end of the strip approached, Fowler attempted to guide the crippled bomber clear along an adjacent taxiway, but without brakes he lost control of the aircraft and it slewed into a number of jeeps before finally coming to rest. One occupant of the jeep was killed; however, the bomb failed to detonate. A later investigation found that Fowler had lost the Beaufort's pneumatic brakes as the result of ground fire damaging part of the air-filled system.

Frank and the crew were to take part in their final, fateful mission on March 13th. Flying Beaufort A9-650, they were tasked to attack the village of Milak and were flying as 'Number 3' of the lead flight. They now had nearly a hundred missions to their credit and were destined for Australia within weeks. Frank was to marry his Kempsey sweetheart, Edith Blight, in early May and the possibility of returning to a normal life was no longer so remote.

The crew had established a sound reputation amongst their peers and Fowler had been rated as "above average" in his most recent assessment as an aircraft commander. The strike on Milak was to be nothing out of the norm. The three flights of bombers would attack the target in line astern at intervals of three-quarters of a mile. Frank's aircraft was seen to proceed and the bomb run was observed as "perfectly normal". Yet at the critical point of bomb released there was a conflagration that swallowed the Beaufort and sent it plunging to the ground with the loss of all lives on board.

The initial debriefing suspected logically that the aircraft was lost to ground fire. However, another Beaufort was lost in an almost identical fashion within the week and was once again witnessed to perish in flames at the point of bomb release. Suspicions arose and a committee was convened to investigate. The tragic truth was that Frank Smith and his close-knit crew had fallen victim to a faulty bomb fuse detonating the 100lb A.S. bombs immediately upon release. It was traced to a poorly designed arming fork on the bombs and subsequent units were recalled and rectified. Unfortunately this finding was too late for Flight Lieutenant Frank Smith and his girl waiting back home.

The remains of the crew were not immediately recoverable as they had fallen in Japanese occupied territory. With the advance of Australian troops they were ultimately laid to rest together nearby, before being re-interred some time later at the Lae War Cemetery along with over 2,000 other servicemen.

The war in the Pacific drew to a close only five months later in August 1945. In the same month, Frank's promotion finally became official and he was made a Flight Lieutenant posthumously. Today a street bears his name in his home town of Kempsey, a country town that he left for the last time over 60 years ago.

The tales of those who go to war are littered with the question "What if?" And Frank Smith is no exception. At only 23 years of age and with so many combat missions behind him, the beginning of Frank's new life was only weeks away when his brave crew were lost. For Flight Lieutenant Frank Smith, one cannot help but think that he was just so close.

In Memory of
Flight Lieutenant FRANCIS OWEN SMITH
422062, Royal Australian Air Force
who died age 23
on 13 March 1945

* Today, the remains of A9-557 have been restored and are displayed at the Australian War Memorial as a tangible and poignant reminder of the contribution of the Australian Beaufort crews.

***

Frank Smith (seated in the Jeep) and his fellow Beaufort crew members. (Photo: E.Blight)

The Beaufort undergoing restoration in the 1990s.

21

GHOSTS

Here they rest. Silent.

Once they were vital warriors surrounded by fire and fury, but now they are at peace. They are objects of curiosity in storage, caught in limbo between the care of conservation and the liberty of the Australian War Memorial's halls. This vast annex is where these treasured relics of combat are preserved for future generations. There are cannons and landing barges, rockets and vehicles, fighters and bombers. All manner of tools of war.

For me, the aircraft hold a special interest. A highly polished Mustang sits beside a weary looking Messerschmitt, the victor beside its spoils. A C-47 Dakota that once carried the body of Australia's wartime leader on his final journey and not far away is the reason that I am here. It is a Beaufort bomber. It's not the most pleasing form an aeroplane has ever taken and "rugged" would probably be the fairest description that could be offered.

Australian-built, its glasshouse nose sits high, while its tailwheel rests on the immaculately clean floor of the hall. The markings of A9-557 still mark the bomber's flanks. Its two large round engines threaten to burst into life, blurt out smoke and noise and send the large three-bladed propellers into a whirring frenzy. But no, like the others, its flying days are now long gone. In fact, its last flight was in 1945 when it crash-landed in New Guinea with one bomb still on board and major systems damaged. It slew off the runway, striking a

Jeep and killing one of the occupants. It then was all but forgotten in the jungle until it was retrieved nearly half a century later.

On that fateful morning, "Jack" Fowler had been at the controls as he had been on 50 other missions, including more than 30 in this very same aircraft. His regular crew was with him too: Geoff Waite (Navigator), John Shipman (Wireless Operator), and Frank Smith (Wireless/Air Gunner). They survived that day, but six weeks later, as their tour of duty neared its end, the experienced aircrew's luck would run out. A bomb would detonate prematurely due to a faulty fuse, engulfing the Beaufort in flames over the village of Maprik.

Now the salvaged A9-557 has come home and is being restored as a tribute to all those who served. The job is nearly done and here she sits, once again a complete, proud aircraft and I walk around her with a silent reverence. In my hand I have a faded photograph of "557", her crew sitting in a Jeep beside her just after a mission, their young faces smiling. There was no way they could know that death's grip was tightening and their lives would end within weeks of the shutter's "click".

I stand back and compare the photograph to the machine before me. My eyes alternate between the black and white picture and the original drab camouflage of the Beaufort as if I can insert those missing lives into the present to complete the scene. It is a pointless exercise as I try to grasp a little less of the airframe and much more of the men who flew her. And then I touch the Beaufort and in that simple act I feel some connection with the crew immediately, for their hands had rested where my hand now rests. A message, WIPE YOUR BOOTS PLEASE, is scrawled near the step on the side of the Beaufort. Little more than graffiti, these letters have survived decades and remind me of the muddy jungle airstrips from which the Beaufort flew.

It's still early in the day and my escort is standing some distance away, allowing me a sense of solitude. The slightest shuffle of feet echoes amongst these proud warriors and I swear that I can almost hear whispers coming from the Beaufort. Voices long past, of boys that were men before their time. In my mind I can see Jack Fowler in the cockpit, Bakelite headsets pulled down tight over his peaked officer's cap.

Further back in the fuselage, Waite and Shipman are busy with their charts and dials. All of them are sweating through their khaki shirts in the tropical heat as the din of the Pratt and Whitney engines drown out any conversation. Glances, nods and thumbs-ups convey so many unspoken words. Together they are moving this bomber ever-closer to the target as they have done so many times before, readying for the strike.

And then there's Frank Smith.

Short, thin and baby-faced. Only 22 years of age, he sits beside the open side-hatch manning the Browning .303 machine gun. Soon he will be back home and marrying an Air Force girl and this blood, sweat and bullets will be a memory. There's a half-smile on his face as he thinks of home. His headsets are pulled down over his sandy hair which is blowing in the slipstream, only inches from where I now perch. He moves inside and ducks his head, climbing into the cramped upper gun-turret towards the aircraft's rear. Almost spherical, the caged transparent ball with two more Browning barrels jutting out at the ready. His young form now visible through the Perspex beside me.

Below, the jungle canopy flies past. Frank scans the heavens and his tail for any fighters that may come their way, but this is 1945 and the Japanese presence in the air is virtually extinct. Even so, he is at the ready and waiting. Waiting for fighters, waiting for the bombs to start falling, waiting for home. He checks his watch and the time-to-target. It is getting close.

Was it Frank who painted the request to "Wipe your feet"? Below the level of the Perspex, a bullet has entered the gun turret through the metal. I move my head and can imagine its trajectory and see its exit point on the far side. How did this bullet not end Frank's life even earlier than fate's ultimately cruel hand? Was he ever scared? I have so many questions, but he cannot see me across the great divide of time and space.

I keep my feet in the same steps he once climbed with my face close to the turret, but it's no use. His baby-faced form is fading. My imagination is no competition for the harsh reality of time and mortality. He lowers his eyes away from the sky and he is gone. All that remains is the cold metal and camouflage. The bare gun barrels and jutting aerials. The bomber's body is still here, but the Beaufort's soul has gone. Will it return in the dark hours when we of the present are tucked up in our beds and lost in our dreams? Do the old warriors climb down from their steeds in battle-dress, shake hands and tell tall tales when no one is around? I hope so.

The office workers are now arriving and my escort shepherds me towards the door. I pause one more time before I leave the presence of the Beaufort and look back. I can see Frank, still with a smile on his face. It is a face I know well, from photographs placed in my home, from my childhood. On mantle pieces on ANZAC Day. For Frank never made it home for the wedding and instead of a church altar my mother stood at a memorial alone, silently crying in the rain. But Frank would never be forgotten.

***

22

A Boeing Baptism

As a young student pilot you dream of the day. As you sweat in the simulator you ponder the day with a degree of trepidation. What will it be like? Will I be up to the task, or will I make a fool of myself? Sooner or later the training must end and reality take the baton. Sooner or later it is time to take to the real sky in a real airliner.

The study had been solid for weeks and the endless scenarios thrown upon me in the simulator had the Boeing 737 feeling more like a torture chamber than an airliner. Day by day I came to know the aircraft better than any other aircraft I had ever flown. From systems knowledge to performance calculations and good old "stick and rudder", the 737 was all I could eat, drink and sleep for the duration of the course. Finally, it was time to stow the books and fly the jet.

To soften our impact on the travelling public, I would first fly the aircraft without passengers in an exercise known as "base training". It consisted of a simple 15-minute flight to a nearby airport followed by a series of circuits and landings, with the only occupants being other trainees just like me. As we scooted across to our destination, the mood amongst the young pilots was mirthful but misleading. We joked about who would crash to earth on their first attempt, while beneath the surface we all prayed that we wouldn't be the offender.

The conversation went quiet as our first comrade took to the skies. There we all sat, in awe, stealing a glimpse of the sky through the open flight deck door and occasionally looking back at the steeply angled aisle. The inertia, noise and gravity were beyond anything that the simulator had valiantly tried to replicate. The occasional sidewards "bunt" in turbulence and the roar of the engines on take-off stirred the adrenalin in every one of us. We had all been passengers before, but never like this. And then there was the change in engine tone followed by a slewing of the airframe. The check captain had failed an engine after take-off and our buddy was sweating his best to maintain control and bring the aircraft back around to land. Then it was the next victim's turn at the helm.

Trainee number one returned to the passenger cabin as number two strapped in. On his way past the galley the former grabbed some food from one of the catering trolleys. His face was white, but a broad grin beamed across his face. It had been a workout, but the experience of a lifetime. A little humour returned and congratulatory jokes were shared as he took his seat and chomped down on a sandwich. The 737 moved off once again.

The sequence was repeated and the engines spooled up with a heartening roar. The brakes were released and we sank back in our seats, rocketing down the runway. The calls of "V1!" and "Rotate!" drifted back from the flight deck as the Boeing's nose rose skyward. And then....*bang!* We all jumped in unison in response to the deafening clang, but still the aircraft climbed away and only a cursory glance came back from the captain", sitting in the flight deck's "jump seat". An instant later we identified the problem; a catering tray had slid out and crashed to the floor. Trainee number one stopped chewing and looked sheepishly sidewards as we burst into muffled laughter.

Back on the ground again there was some head shaking as the tray was stowed and I passed grinning trainee number two on my way to the flight deck. The two captains smiled and made me feel at home as I strapped into the right-hand seat. All of the visual cues were identical to the simulator, from where my seat's edge sat relative to the VHF radios, to my eyeline down the coaming and nose of the aircraft. I felt at home, but with a pulse rate of 120.

My heart rate increased as we turned onto the runway and the broad white dotted centreline extended into the distance. Unlike the simulator, I now felt how high I was actually sitting above the ground compared to the Barons and Chieftains that I had cut my teeth on. "What must it look like from a 747?" I pondered momentarily, not knowing that I would find out one day. With my mind focused back on the job at hand, my pulse actually slowed, as I became consumed with what I had been trained to do and nothing else. A check of the windsock, a radio call from the left-hand seat, and we were on our way.

I pressed the button in front of the thrust levers and they came to life beneath my hand. The captain then rested his hand on the levers as the decision to go or stop now rested with him. I concentrated on keeping the jet straight and acknowledging the call of "80 Knots!" as our decision speed loomed. "V-1!" he called, taking his hands from the thrust levers as I raised my left hand to join the right on the yoke. "Rotate!"

I eased the yoke back towards myself smoothly and the 737 leapt into the sky. I counted in my head to keep the rate of the nose rising steady until we were climbing away. The call of "Positive Rate!" came from beside me and I responded with "Gear up!" This was it, I was flying. No simulation, no "position freeze" and no way out. The earth was behind me and my career was ahead of me and somehow I still managed a smile.

In an instant, it was time to wheel the airliner to the left and into the circuit pattern. Autothrottle off and I lowered the nose at 1,500 feet before calling for checklists without delay. Check, check, check, my mind switched from accelerating into flight to preparing to land. The runway's landing threshold past by and the clock was running. Landing gear down, flaps extended and more checklists to complete as I turned towards the airfield once more.

Aligned with the centreline and with all of the checklists completed, the task was now to land 50 tons of metal and a handful of souls. Aim point, airspeed, centreline; I was fine tuning the approach as we descended ever lower. Still, doubt creeps into the mind of every new pilot...."Don't spoil this with a bad landing". I tried to silence the voice with ordered thoughts but it stayed there niggling me until about 100 feet above the ground when my concentration could've silenced an artillery barrage.

The picture out of the window looked good as I eased back on the thrust levers and teased back on the control column. Just as I contemplated making an adjustment, *thump*, and we were on the ground. My left hand slid forward and raised the reverse thrust levers, causing the engines to scream in protestation and me to heave forward in my harness. *Keep straight, slow down and stow the "reversers"*. I was still pushing the brake pedals through the floor when the captain reached over to shake my hand. I couldn't believe that I'd done it after all of the training. I smiled and grabbed his firm hand with my sweaty grip. "Let's go again," he chirped, as if we had an unlimited ride ticket on a rollercoaster. And we sort of did.

The second circuit was slower than the first, or perhaps my brain had just advanced up the aisle from seat 15A and into the flight deck. Another reasonable circuit and a slightly better landing, but it was obvious to me that competency on a consistent basis would only come with more time and effort. As we taxied back to the runway's end for my final circuit, I was briefed by the captain that we would leave the landing gear extended for this circuit. This was a good sign as it meant my first two attempts had cleared me for the final challenge: An engine failure after takeoff. Leaving the wheels down was meant to degrade the climb performance of this empty aeroplane to simulate a single-engined climb out a little more realistically.

Eighty knots-V1-Rotate...here we go again. However, this time, when the landing gear was retracted, I noted the captain moving an A4-sized checklist to hover over the thrust levers and conceal the identity of which engine he was about to reduce to idle power. And then he did it.

The Boeing yawed to the right and I blocked it with the left rudder. *Block it and lock it* I thought to myself, as any foot movement would have me chasing my tail and the jet rocking about the sky. I held it steady, checked my speed and headed for the heavens. Unlike a real engine failure when we would conduct a number of checklists and reconfigure a number of associated systems, we simply turned back into the circuit with one engine at idle and the landing gear lowered. We crunched the numbers for a partial flap setting of "Flaps 15" and I prepared for my first single engined approach and landing.

By this circuit, my brain was keeping pace with the workload and a good deal of my trepidation was now calmed. I was busy, but surviving, and I'll take that as a rookie pilot on his first day out. As the runway now sat ahead with all checklists completed, I forced myself to sit up straight and ward off any tendency to slump. I also reminded myself that "Flaps 15" is almost in the correct attitude for landing and there won't be much rearward force needed on the control column as I flare. Still, as the runway drew closer at this slightly higher approach speed, I got a little gun shy and checked back on the yoke just a touch. Nothing much, a nervous twitch, but enough to result in the aircraft floating a little and touching down further into the runway than I wanted. Damn it!

My self-recrimination escaped the two captains on the flight deck. We taxied clear of the runway and again the captain shook my hand

and congratulated me. The next trainee was already on his way as I left the flight deck, half-stunned that I had apparently made the grade. Then the grin started at the corner of my mouth and spread across my face like a wildfire. I shook hands with the other rookies and took my seat in the cabin, as happy as I can ever remember being.

I looked out the window as we moved off for another three circuits under someone else's hand, still smiling. This was my first taste of the 737 and my world was forever changed. I wondered if I would ever appear as confident and relaxed as the captain that sat beside me. For the moment, I was happy to just keep learning and listening, for my life in the airlines was only just beginning and this was merely a baptism.

***

23

TESTING TIMES

From time to time, aircraft can be stripped back to the bone. This can occur routinely for scheduled maintenance, sometimes in the process of a loving restoration and, on other occasions, in the wake of major damage. Whatever the reason may be, once the aircraft is finally reassembled and the engineers have put their signatures to the completed work, it is time to fly once more.

In many cases, before the fare-paying public are taken aloft in the reborn machine, it falls upon company pilots to make the first flight after maintenance. These flights are seen as a blessing for some and treated with trepidation by others. There are pilots who relish the opportunity to really fly the aeroplane without the constraints of air routes or passengers and there are those who dread being the first to take the aircraft back into the sky. As with all things in life, it's a case of horses for courses.

For me, post-maintenance test flights were a joy as a young flight instructor. As much as I enjoyed my time tutoring new pilots, the amount of hands-on flying time could be limited. It was easy to become an expert at talking about flying while your own skills quietly eroded. I always made sure that I demonstrated various exercises and kept my hand in, but flying time from the left-hand seat rarely eventuated.

The flights called for a certain sequence of manoeuvres and power settings to be checked off pro forma to verify that the aircraft was once again performing as it should. The flights were quite thorough and a lot of fun, but my strongest memory is of the first of these flights that I ever conducted. I had spoken with the engineers, meticulously examined the relevant documentation and inspected the aeroplane externally, but when I climbed on board the little single-engined Piper I was taken aback. Thoroughly lashed down in the baggage compartment was a milk crate filled with aircraft parts! These parts weren't just screws and light bulbs, there were gudgeon pins and con rods.

I climbed down off the wing and made my way back to the engineers with the milk crate under my arm. They seemed to be anticipating my arrival and my obvious question about the inventory I was carrying. Their explanation was that these were parts "left over" after the rebuild and that they needed to be carried to ensure that the aeroplane's weight-and-balance specifications conformed to the flight manual. There were wry grins all round as this was standard procedure to test the rookie pilot before he set about testing the aircraft. Similarly, I had the same joke played upon me years later prior to a post-maintenance check in a Boeing 737.

A few years later, I enjoyed another series of flights, but this time they were new aeroplanes freshly delivered from France. They were a mix of Socata TB10 Tobagos and TB20 Trinidads, and at the time they were proving popular aircraft with flying schools and private owners alike. However, when they first landed in the country, many still had the various ancillary switches labelled in French and some even still bore French registration markings on their flanks.

As part of their certification in their new home, all of these switches and their actions had to be verified and relabelled and the aircraft subsequently test-flown. Again, the parameters of the flight were guided by a list of tasks, but again the flights were tremendous fun. Each aircraft had that new car smell and the engines purred without a ripple as I swept about over the open fields of the nearby training area. It was a wonderful opportunity to both fly a new aircraft and really gain a better knowledge of its workings, having regularly visited the hangar as they underwent their various inspections and reassembly.

My first post-maintenance flight in an airliner befell me because of my proximity to the airport, I suspect. My phone rang in the early hours asking if I could be at the airport at 5am to meet the 737 fleet manager to fly an aircraft that had undergone major work on its tailplane. I lived only 20 minutes from the airport so I knew that I could make it in time and I was excited at gaining the opportunity. However, as I drove to the airport my excitement was tempered a little.

It was a period when a rare shadow had been cast over the 737 in the wake of fatal accidents. US Air Flight 427 had recently crashed, killing 132 people, and the mysteriously lost United Airlines 585 had resurfaced. From the ensuing investigations, it was suspected that there were problems with the 737's tailplane, or more specifically its rudder. It was subsequently found that in both accidents the rudder power control unit was suspected of causing a "hard over", driving the rudder in the opposite direction to the pilot's control inputs. However, as I drove to the airport that morning, this still wasn't known.

There was a great deal of discussion about the accidents and possible rudder issues, and operational memos were circulating thick and fast. Pilots were got jumpy every time they struck wake turbulence on the approach to land, as this was also suspected to have been a factor at the time. Now I was about to go flying in a 737 that had just had the tail section pulled apart.

The atmosphere in the hangar was quite serious by normal standards and there was no milk crate of spare parts to lighten the mood. We checked the documentation and the aircraft and readied it for the flight. The senior engineer who had signed off on the aircraft would accompany us in what was more a gesture of morale than a crewing requirement. As soon as the rising sun and airport curfew permitted, the three of us taxied out and departed over the coast, clear of habitation.

Out over the ocean, we levelled off and the captain disconnected the autopilot. He proceeded to run through all manner of tasks with an emphasis on the flight controls. The time then came to switch off the 3,000 psi hydraulic system that drove the controls in a procedure known as a "manual reversion". The captain was now controlling the aeroplane without any power assistance and solely from the control column via the cables that ran through the 737 to the wings and tail.

The manual reversion calls for degrees of both strength and anticipation. The control surfaces are now being deflected into the force of the 250-knot airstream. Furthermore, as the movement of the controls was far slower and laboured, any change in attitude, or rolling out of a turn, had to be initiated far earlier than normal to have effect. After a series of climbs, descents and turns, it became apparent that all of the items on the form had been met and we were free to return home. However, before the hydraulic system was switched back on, the captain looked at me and asked if I'd like to fly the aeroplane in manual reversion. I said that I would.

I had flown a manual reversion in the simulator, but as they say, "There's nothing like the real thing". To feel the weight of the controls in my hands and to appreciate first-hand just how much lag occurred in flying the jet was a lesson that I hold close to this day, and I am indebted to the captain for offering me the experience. Still, after the hydraulic system was restored and the controls returned to normal, he offered me one last exercise; a rapid descent.

Again, the rapid descent is practised in the simulator, but hopefully never flown in the aeroplane. It is aimed to descend the aircraft down into the lower levels of oxygen-rich air in a minimum of time in the event of a cabin depressurisation. Our oxygen and pressurisation system was working fine, so he wanted me to close the thrust levers, lower the nose and descend at the maximum speed of 340 knots. The descent was made even steeper by deploying the speed brake, which raises panels on the wings to disturb the air flow and the lift that is generated by the wings.

A couple of hours before, I was sleeping soundly in my bed, and now I was spearing back down to earth faster than I had ever done before. The airspeed hovered near the red markings and threatened to sound an "overspeed" warning at any moment as the altimeter wound down like a crazed clock. The noise of the rushing air was substantial and added to the event as I looked down at the ocean from a very different perspective. Passing 12,000 feet, I stowed the speedbrake and gradually raised the nose so that life returned to normal by the time we reached 10,000 feet. All was in order and my pulse was still racing a little from pure enjoyment at really flying my aeroplane.

After such an eventful flight, the approach and landing seemed a formality, although I reminded myself that this was the very situation when complacency can creep in and ruin an otherwise great day. The mood was very different when we returned to the flight-line and the other engineers boarded the aeroplane. There was an air of a job well done and it was a tremendous opportunity to interact with the men and women that work so brilliantly to keep our aircraft flying. For the first time that day a few jokes were exchanged and the spectre of the rudder hard-overs was not at the forefront of our thoughts. It had been a day to remember.

All aircraft need to be stripped down and put back together at some time in their life. Even though modern aircraft are magnificently built, it is the only way to truly monitor what is going on beneath the surface after extended periods of time. When this occurs, someone will be asked to fly the aircraft before commercial operations can resume. The opportunity to fly these sorties is well worthwhile and constitute some of the most memorable flights that I have undertaken. Still, if you are asked to fly an aircraft fresh from the workshop, don't be surprised if you find a milk crate of spare parts waiting for you.

***

24

YOU, ME AND A TIGER MAKES THREE

They say that every journey begins with a single step. Well this journey began with a great degree of doubt and conflicting information. The weather forecast told a tale of woe and wild wet winds, but as I looked out my kitchen window to the south, the sky was clear and the stars were twinkling. Hmmm, what was one to do?

My wife, Kirrily, and I had planned to fly our antique Tiger Moth biplane from our home to an air show across the border in Queensland. It was not the simplest of day-trips as it called for us to cover over 500 miles in an aeroplane that travelled at around 80 miles an hour. Six hours in an open cockpit armed with goggles and a leather helmet is a blink for the pioneering aviators of yesteryear, but it is still a fair hop in the 21st century on a cold winter's day.

As we compared the lines of the encoded weather forecast to charts and satellite photos, we agreed that the weather was coming, but it wasn't here yet. Furthermore, the front was moving at about 30 miles an hour, so if we took off ahead of it, we should be able to stay that way. With a plan formulated, we made our way to the airfield, loaded our limited luggage into the small locker behind the rear cockpit and readied to depart as the dawn's light was peering through the mist.

As Kirrily sat at the ready, I flicked the switches and grasped the brass edge of my old wooden propeller. Feeling a slight resistance, I pulled downward and flicked the engine into life. The *pop-pop pop-pop* of the four cylinders defied the cold of the morning and soon the propeller formed a walnut disc in the new sunlight. I pulled the wheel chocks away from the tyres and stowed them before lumbering up onto the wing and into the cockpit. Our attire was bulky as Kirrily and I both knew how cool a flight in the Tiger Moth could be. Layers of thermal underwear, long johns, jeans, shirt, polar fleece vest, flying suit, scarf and leather jacket cocooned us, while the four straps of the harness lashed us tightly into the cockpit.

As I increased the power and started to taxi, the slipstream from the spinning blades cast back additional airflow that still managed to creep down beyond our scarves. We were chilled after only two minutes and bid haste to the sun and the warmth it would bring. Like us, the engine was slow to rise in temperature so we sat waiting at the runway's edge with one eye to the south looking for the predicted weather to emerge.

The time had come and I lined up on the runway, swinging the small tailwheel around behind me. Without further ado I advanced the throttle and the old 1930s instruments vibrated into life. As the airspeed increased I raised the tail from the runway, offering a little better forward vision from the rear cockpit. And then the Tiger told me it was time to fly and I eased her into the air with a gentle rearward force on the control stick.

That point of liftoff is always endearing in an old aeroplane as you feel every bump as the wind whistles through the bracing wires between the wings. There is no roaring into the wide blue yonder, just a gentle chugging into the sky at a speed not far removed from a Sunday afternoon drive. One after the other, familiar homes, roads and tress passed us by as we clawed our way to a friendly altitude and friendlier winds pushing us towards our destination.

By now the sun sits warmly out to our right above the Pacific Ocean as I keep the highway beneath me as my primary navigation reference. I dawdle off to the right to give the parachute jump zone a wide berth before turning back to the road and carrying on. It's flying at its most basic, nothing too complicated and nothing too stressful. Kirrily and I do possess the luxury of an intercom that allows us to chat as we fly. We take turns at guiding the Tiger northward and rolling left and right to take a closer look at a homestead or a small boat out on the reservoir.

We fly by a tall orange-and-white radio tower, then the airport where we first met and the city in which we lived before we retreated to our semi-rural life. We weave our way through the narrow corridor for light aircraft, although a few of the landmarks have changed since we both taught student pilots to navigate the same route years before. Free of the city and the restrictions of its airspace, we climb higher and the landscape spreads out before us in all its glory.

At this pace, everything is leisurely and each puff of turbulence evokes a gentle rumble through the wood and fabric of the Tiger Moth. Maps are checked and, from time to time, Kirrily's gloved hand appears, pointing to some feature below or another aircraft out for a "morning stroll". Next, the vineyards begin to appear and soon we are gently touching down on the grass field where the Tiger Moth was restored a few years before.

We wander past the antique petrol bowsers and oil signs into the hangar which houses other Tigers that are yet to rise for the day. We share a coffee in a well-worn cup with Ray, the man that brought our Tiger back to life from little more than a forgotten airframe. The community that surrounds the world of old aeroplanes is far reaching and its language spans the oceans. The temptation is to talk all day, but the weather is definitely coming as we receive word that it is now raining at the airfield from which we departed two hours earlier.

Ray lends a hand, swinging our propeller into life and this time we set course over rich green rolling paddocks and livestock having their morning feed. We could be over the English countryside or have been transported through time. Wrapped in our 70-year-old aeroplane there is nothing in the air or on the ground to offer us a reference to our time or place. We might be here, or we might be then. Our own tiny time machine.

We now choose to follow a railway line and do so at only 500 feet as the rules dictate. A train coming the other way flashes his headlight and I waggle our wings. The train is all silver with a blue stripe; perhaps this is the 1950s. But then the present rushes up in the form of a pair of Hornet jet fighters, their arrival broadcast over the radio. They are the reason we tread along the rail-lines at only a few hundred feet – a military air base is nearby.

Whack....Whack!

One, then another, crosses our path like finned bullets. They are gone before their sound arrives and it is a noise that pierces my old leather helmet. If I had blinked I wouldn't have seen them, but I had and they were spectacular. I contemplate how much chaos a single fighter jet could have caused in the First World War when battles were fought in the sky in frail machines like my Tiger. It would have been no contest but it's an intriguing scenario nonetheless.

We continue wending our way over farms and below the hill-line, edging ever closer to the coast. We pass my mother's hometown and I know her friends are keeping watch for the red-and-silver biplane to pass overhead, which we do with a large sweeping turn over the district before leaving the dairy farms for the beaches.

The sun has now passed overhead and the airflow has made its way through our fabric armour and chilled us to the core. The waves crash and then ripple up the beaches below, but hunger is beginning to grab our attention. I checked my watch and it is less than an hour until our next landing. Then we could fuel the Tiger and eat.

Our next landing is at a major airport that is home to airliners and charter aircraft. The air traffic controller keeps us out of each other's way and soon we are rolling up to the bowser to replenish the Tiger's tanks. We ready the aircraft for departure before we sit at a bench and consume our well-travelled sandwiches and drink tea from our Thermos. I'm hungrier than I realised because these are the best ham sandwiches I've ever tasted.

We enjoy a conversation without the background of the roaring Gipsy Major motor and the air rushing by. We clasp our cups of tea in both hands in an effort to warm our fingers and we allow the rising vapours to heat our chins. With one more leg to fly, the weather has been left behind but the short winter day threatens to steal our sunlight. Once more I swing the propeller, and we both strap in and take to the skies.

For the remaining hours I simply keep Australia to my left and the Pacific Ocean to my right, with a yellow strip of coastline running beneath the Tiger. People on the beach stop and look skyward, their attention captured by the uncharacteristic sound of the old unmuffled motor. Some wave and kids run in small circles leaving patterns on the sand. We respond with our wings and a wave and that simple interaction warms us both a little.

Mile by mile our destination draws closer. Queensland's capital city sits out from our wing tip as we continue our coastal trek, out of the way of the "big boys" flying in and out of town. Finally, we draw abeam Kirrily's parents hometown and turn west over the bay towards them. The lowering sun and the fine mist of oil on our goggles and windscreens prove an impediment to locating the airfield at first. Then Kirrily's gloved hand appears again, pointing slightly off to the left of the nose, and we are have arrived.

We peel off overhead and can see her parents' car parked beside my friend's hangar where our Tiger is to sleep. A few kangaroos loiter threateningly along the edge of the runway, grazing in the twilight. The moon is now beginning to rise over the ocean, a bright orange ball, while its alter ego is still to set. Perched between day and night, I guide the Tiger down for one last descent as the windsock flaps lightly.

As the ground grows closer, I reduce the power and pull back on the control stick slightly. Sitting proudly, tail-low and nose-high, the Tiger wafts down towards the grass runway until the rumble and bump confirm that we have arrived. Birds circle overhead and the kangaroos hold their ground, staring at us as we taxi clear of the runway towards the hangar.

After more than seven hours aloft, we park the Tiger and bring the propeller to a standstill. Switches off and checklists complete, we raise our goggles and peel the helmets from our heads. The smiles of family and friends warm us far more than the thermals and long johns as we clamber down from the wing to hugs and handshakes. It has been a long day, but worth every ounce of effort.

After wiping down her sides, we push the Tiger into the hangar and switch off the lights. She now sat silently among strangers, other craft of the skies, though not quite so old. Later, as we sit back and exchange stories of jet fighters and silver trains, was there also quiet conversation in the darkened confines of the hangar between the aeroplanes, I wonder? Tall tales and true of towering cumulus and ham-fisted pilots? Whispered words that no aviator was ever destined to hear? Personally, I'd like to think so.

***

25

FIRE IN THE SKY

The devastation was nothing new. Bushfires have been ravaging Australia since time began and these current outbreaks had been going for days, but now they were getting close. Really close.

While my family and home were not in danger, the local airfield sat a distance out of town, surrounded by the beauty of bushland. At most times the setting was a blessing, a place to escape where like-minded folks huddled in hangars and told tall tales and true. Today was very different as the pall of dark grey smoke hung over head and the fire-front crept ever closer.

The sound of fire-fighting aircraft was a blend of thumping rotors and roaring engines as they transited the sky overhead. From dams to the fires and back again they shuttled their precious cargo of water in their bellies or slung beneath their skids in massive buckets. Fire trucks raced along the roadways and barricades were set up to isolate the fire from the population. A sunny Saturday afternoon was rapidly becoming dire and the airfield was clearly under threat.

All the while my aircraft sat in the hangar, despite being particularly vulnerable. For, not only was my aircraft filled to the brim with fuel, it was an antique deHavilland Tiger Moth biplane. Its flesh was fabric and its frame a mixture of a metal tube fuselage and wooden wings. There were no doors to lock, only a simple canvas cover draped over the two open cockpits that sat one behind the other. Even the instrument panels were crafted from timber. My beloved aeroplane was a tinder box filled with flammable fuel.

The fire did not even need to reach the airfield to threaten the Tiger Moth. The smoke was filled with glowing red embers, whipped into a frenzy on the gusty north-westerly wind. One ember beneath the hangar's eaves, one ember on the fragile fabric and the "Tiger" could smoulder and erupt. It was a thought that did not sit comfortably with me as I arranged tables for a charity function I was attending.

I monitored the reports until it was no use and decided to move the Tiger before it was too late. A good friend, Vern, offered to drive me to the airfield, but the journey was thwarted by a barricade and fire-fighters on watch. After negotiations, they agreed to let us proceed, but only if Vern turned around and returned with due haste. We agreed and made a beeline to the airfield.

The hangar doors groaned open and we pulled the biplane out into the open. I had left the aircraft ready to fly after my last flight, so I carried out an external inspection and confirmed that she was still full of fuel and oil. I climbed into the cockpit and strapped in, flicking a magneto switch and giving Vern the "all clear" to swing the propeller by hand. Thankfully the spark caught the fuel vapour the first time and the Gipsy Major engine burst into life with a belch and a puff of smoke.

I flicked the other magneto switch and Vern pulled the wheel chocks clear as the engine settled into its steady rhythm. There was nothing else to do, so Vern hopped back into his car and drove off towards the fire-fighters' checkpoint. Meanwhile, I ran through my checks and "engine run" with one eye on the instruments and one on the approaching wall of smoke. There was no time to lose, but there was no sense in rushing either, so when both the Tiger Moth and me were ready, I lined up on the runway. Stick back, I opened the throttle and we were away. Soon after, I relaxed the back pressure on the stick and the tail rose from the ground as the aeroplane signalled to me that it wanted to fly. Just a few moments and a few knots more and it was time. I gently eased her into the sky and away from the looming danger.

For all of the cloud to the north, the way was clear to the south and east. There was scorched earth off one wingtip and rolling green paddocks and the ocean off the other. Another airfield sat a mere 20 miles away on the coast and my plan was to hold midway between the two until I could see how the day was to play out. I was buffeted by thermals and gusts as the confused air swirled about me. As I climbed to altitude it began to calm down and cool and I was struck by a certain smell. Open cockpit aeroplanes are prone to the smell of fuel, oil and combustion riding the slipstream and into the nostrils, but this was different.

The normal odour of mechanisation was dominated by the smell of the burning bush as grass and eucalypts were vapourised and belched into the atmosphere. The smell drove deep into the nasal passages, although my goggles prevented the eye-watering sting that would no doubt have resulted. As I climbed ever higher I could see long advancing lines of orange flames racing to join up and the valiant fire crews wedged between them battling the union. Their red trucks looked like toys at the base of the towering smoke plumes, and yet somehow they were holding this mighty force at bay.

The earpieces in my leather helmet filled with the chatter of the airborne assault as one aircraft after another either attacked the blaze or protected properties with pinpoint precision. I circled in the distance with the security of the coastal airfield behind me while these faceless voices made pass after pass, each releasing a plume of water or brightly coloured retardant at the critical moment. They would then speed away to refill and return.

From my removed vantage point at 4,000 feet I was witness to the amazing choreography being played out in the distance. Even so, at that altitude the smoke-front still towered above me like a line of ash-filled thunderstorms. In places, the smoke was dense black rolls, while in other areas it mushroomed in expanding pillars of light grey, depending on what fuel they were consuming. The sheer power and violence of nature made me feel both miniscule and useless as I orbited miles away from any danger.

Below me the earth dropped away to the coastline at a jagged angle. The rocky escarpment had water creeping down its face and I couldn't help but wonder how that water would be so precious only a few miles away. The lush green bushland at the base of the cliff and the sandy beaches beyond were juxtaposed with the life-and-death battle taking place to the north. There, wildlife was perishing in vast numbers and bushland vanished with every wind change.

As the sun sank a little lower, the horizon took on an orange hue and the few distant clouds assumed pinkish tones. The smoke had brought with it a setting sun that was both beautiful and at odds with its deadly origins. The wind also abated with the lengthening shadows and the fire-fighters gained the upper hand for the first time. The radio chatter settled down and the scurrying aircraft were replaced by methodical, unhurried sweeps. My home airfield was no longer in danger and it was safe for me to descend once more.

As I did so, the smell of the smoke again became more intense, although now there was no buffeting breeze. I joined the circuit pattern and the Gipsy motor chugged as it is prone to do as it idles. I could hear the wind in the wings' bracing wires and feel it brush against my cheek as I slipped the Tiger down towards the runway. Still, fire trucks and flashing red beacons could be seen speeding along the roads.

Coming to a halt outside my hangar, I silenced the Tiger with the final flick of the magneto switches. On the apron and inside the hangar there was a coating of fine ash on the floor and a variety of dry leaves, their edges singed. The fire had not made it within miles and yet the debris of the bushfire was everywhere to be seen. The threat had passed for now, but even as I stood there small particles stung my eyes.

These fires will continue to form a part of the bushland's cycle of life and even the most charred regions will eventually regenerate. As a younger man I had fought the fires and seen them close up, at ground level. However, that afternoon that I spent perched between two airfields in an antique biplane gave me a new understanding. It gave me an appreciation of the vertical reach and broad base of the fire that could only be gained from an elevated platform. At 4,000 feet I not only witnessed the fire's power, but the surrounding terrain and the real life-and-death battle of the men, women and machines that fight the flames. They are the true heroes when there is fire in the sky.

***

The Tiger Moth.

Shining in the Sun. A Boeing 737.

26

A WORLD CHANGED

Bruce and I arrived at the airport prior to sunrise only to find that our straightforward sequence of one sector flying and one sector as a passenger had been brutally rearranged. The day would still see us making it home, but far after five more hours of flying than had been scheduled. However, by the time the sun had risen again, this inconvenience would seem very, very small.

By the time I made it home that night I was exhausted. It had been a long day compounded by the spectre of unemployment floating over my head. Everywhere I turned it seemed like there was a new report on the imminent collapse of the airline I flew for. Even as I walked through the terminal to the aircraft, the newsagent posters reminded me of the dire peril my company was facing and it took a conscious effort to keep my head up and smile at the waiting passengers.

On board there were still more headlines on the papers laid out neatly in the galley while the aircraft log books were quickly filling with an increasing number of permissible unserviceabilities. Spare parts were growing harder to come by and engineers were struggling to make do under their own looming storm clouds. There had even been a company memo informing crew that meals would no longer be provided on board. Even so, morale amongst the employees remained high amid the gloom, but the ongoing uncertainty was wearing thin.

Back at home, after dinner, I resisted the inclination to fall asleep in front of the television and instead showered and climbed into bed at an early hour. I was asleep in minutes and never heard my wife, Kirrily, come to bed three hours later. Even when the phone rang, I somehow integrated it into my dream and it seemed absolutely logical for the ringing sound to be coming from the amplifiers at a Rolling Stones concert. The nudging of my wife didn't integrate so well and was met with aggrieved disorientation. Slowly I focused and eased myself up on one elbow and watched Kirrily as she nodded with her ear to the phone and fumbled to find the television's remote control with her other hand. Then she turned to me and simply stated, "They're flying aircraft into buildings in New York".

She had hung up the phone and the screen now came to life with ticker tape text across the bottom and the sight of the smoking Twin Towers in their death throes. It was almost too great a scene to process, particularly when my first mental image was that of a small wayward Cessna bouncing off a building and not an airliner. The devastation was immense and the billowing pillars of smoke confirmed that it must have been a substantial aeroplane that had collided with the buildings. But *two* buildings? How was this possible?

It was midnight in Australia and as fragments of information were conveyed it became increasingly apparent that this was not an accident. The true horror of the United States under attack was sinking in and I wondered how many more aircraft were being used as manned missiles as I braced for more tragic news. Was this a full-scale assault I was witnessing, and at what point would it cease? For God's sake there were people leaping from windows to their death as the world watched gasping.

Shocked, stunned and confused, we watched the broadcasts and flicked between channels until fatigue finally wore us down and we fell asleep. Even when we woke the next morning, we turned on the television to confirm that we hadn't shared some horrific nightmare. Sections of New York were rubble, the Pentagon bore a gaping wound and, near Pittsburgh, a Boeing 757 had hurtled into the ground leaving little more than a crater. Our world was forever changed.

Over the ensuing days, many of our fellow pilots were grounded in the United States, while at home we wrestled with what had actually happened. We debated with what it would mean for global aviation now that one of man's most towering technological achievements had been turned into a weapon of war. Any way that the events 9-11 were examined, there was nothing but tragedy and bad news. By comparison, the fate of my airline seemed both irrelevant and sealed. In an industry facing a global meltdown, I knew my company did not have the resources to evade falling off the precipice. Still, compared to the genuine suffering that was taking place elsewhere, I found it rather selfish to worry about job security.

True to my suspicions, the news for the airline grew progressively worse to the degree that the media were now nominating which day it would close its doors. The managers continued to speak defiantly and even as Kirrily and I drove to the airport that Friday morning at 3am, the company was telling me that it was business as usual.

She dropped me off outside the terminal little before 5am and made her way to her own aircraft at the terminal of my airline's prime competitor where she was a pilot. Straight away I was aware that something was not right, as a group of passengers had gathered outside the large glass doors, unable to gain entry. I joined them in waving at the sensor, but the automatic doors would not budge. I then caught the eye of a security guard inside the terminal who walked over, pointed at me and then pointed again to the far end of the terminal where the valet car park was located.

Somewhat embarrassed, I left the stranded passengers and made my way as I'd been instructed before the same security guard granted me access through a small door. I was advised that the airline was no more, and escorted to the pilot's crew room. Here I was supervised as I emptied my letterbox of company mail before being escorted back to from whence I came and onto the sidewalk. There were no water cannons from fire trucks and no final parking of the brakes as I had envisaged there would be at the end of my service with the company; just an ignominious administrative process that was over in minutes. The sun had still not risen and I stood in the dark – unemployed and pondering what would come next.

I did not ponder for long. Instead I walked to retrieve our car from the "enemy's" car park and drove to the nearby metropolitan airport where I had worked as a charter pilot and flight instructor many years before. As I sat on the doorstep of a flying school, I called my fellow airline mates to give them notice of what had transpired through the night and that they were now without a job. I was still on the phone as the sun rose and the staff began to filter in. On recognising a familiar face I seized the moment and, within a few minutes, I had a hot cup of coffee and a couple of days of flight theory instruction each week. My lot in life was definitely not that bad.

For the rest of the day the news of the airline's collapse shared the headlines with the ongoing fallout from the events of 9-11. Footage of uniformed employees congregating outside the locked terminal buildings across Australia alternated with the still-horrific scenes of the smoking Twin Towers in New York. Over and over they showed the moment when the sleek jets slammed into the buildings' flanks. My world *and the* world had been turned on their heads in less than a week and uncertainty was the shared emotion.

I began applying for full-time work and righting the ship that had been my career. The government employment agency looked at my detailed resume only to tell me that I was "highly skilled, but totally unemployable". After a few weeks without regular work, there were days when I kicked my flight bag across the room in frustration, but generally I was better behaved. Just as my time as a paramedic years before had taught me to appreciate every single day that I was breathing, the global events of 9-11 gave me perspective on my own minimal woes.

Finally I found my way back onto the flight deck, however this time I was to cross the globe rather than the country. My first flight with my new airline took me to Paris, and as I sat in a cafe on the Champs-Elysees one sunny Saturday morning, the events of recent months seemed very distant, though at the same time they were never far away. In Charles de Gaulle Airport, heavily armed men intermingled with passengers, while occasionally a distant *thud* could be heard. The sound of unattended baggage being detonated, I was told.

Everywhere that I travelled, aviation had become a focal point for all of the wrong reasons. Flight deck doors were now bulletproof and guarded by cameras and secret codes and passwords. Security guards at checkpoints patted down flight crews and anything as dangerous as nail clippers had become contraband. Air travel had lost its innocence and everyone associated with it was a suspect.

The situation did not improve with events such as the "Shoe Bomber" and the threat of surface-to-air missile attacks at London's Heathrow Airport. Flying out of London at the height of tensions, airport roads had checkpoints and military vehicles replaced taxis outside the terminal. The following New Year's Eve, as we taxied at New York's JFK Airport it was wrapped in a cloak of apparent darkness as the big jets all moved anonymously without their coloured tail-fins illuminated. Every jet that night climbed away from the earth with as much performance as their engines could provide.

Like the world, aviation was now divided into two categories; the days before and after 9-11. In many ways we all longed for the old times, but we also knew that they were gone forever. The view from the flight deck remained equally spectacular as we still descended upon brilliant city skylines by night and watched in awe as the first rays of dawn eked their way above the horizon. Beneath our wings, the way in which aviation operated across the oceans or even at rural airports would never be the same. It was true that certain freedoms had been replaced by stringent procedures and vigilance had consumed the idle gaze. However, if we cared to persevere, the magic of flight still remained and our world was still a place of diverse beauty, despite the efforts of those who sought to tear it down.

***

27

A Sacred Site

I am midway through my solo flight around Australia and every day presents new beauties beyond my imagination. Today has been a long day and, with a good many miles behind me, the final run is now 170 miles along the Western Australian coast, beginning with the beautiful Shark Bay. With full tanks of fuel, sandy beaches below and clear skies above, I decide to fly at least part of this last stage at the relatively low altitude of 500 feet above ground level. At 500 feet AGL, the detail in the scenery below becomes even more acute, with individual trees and even leaves, easily discernible.

The world seems to pass by more quickly at this height and abandoned airstrips and dirt tracks come and go in a heartbeat. All the while, the white sands are a constant companion out to my right-hand side, with waves gently lapping the shore on isolated beaches. My mind has almost exceeded capacity, absorbing the broad spectrum of colours and textures that I have seen today – and this coastal fringe provides even more. I want to yell the praises of this region to the world, but then wonder if the key to its beauty lies in its isolation and sparse spattering of mankind.

Almost on cue, the remnants of past habitation slip by beneath me; a ghost town. I wheel the Jabiru around and look down along the line of the wing which seems to point at the structures below me. I guess it was once a thriving community of miners or farmers, now long gone. The buildings remain, blending back into the outback sands out of which they grew. Corrugated tin roofing flapping in the breeze and empty door frames, open to the drifting sands. Only the stone walls seem to offer any resistance to the onslaught of time and nature.

From above, they stand so alone and yet undoubtedly played host to hilarity, hope and heartache in grander times. All around, the eye can see nothing but the horizon; still these pioneers staked their claim in this very spot. Now many undoubtedly lie in tiny graves on the small ridge a few miles up the road. I cannot help but wonder what stories those stone walls might tell if they could speak. The sound of my engine fades too, as I level the wings and head south to Kalbarri.

The land ahead now begins to rise to meet me and I decide that is time to place some distance between the earth and my aircraft once again. As I track slightly inland, the beaches are gradually replaced by foliage and ridge lines whose profiles are becoming accentuated by the afternoon sun. I am now "laying off" quite an amount of drift to counter the strong wind that is blowing, and I notice a discernible change in my speed across the ground. It has been a long day and my eyes are weary as I scan my chart to locate my lodgings for the night at Murchison Station. It lies on a bend in the river to the north of the airport, so I decide to follow the Murchison River that now looms large ahead.

Without difficulty, I sight the few buildings that constitute the historic station and orbit overhead as requested to notify them of my arrival. Confident that I have made enough noise to attract their attention, I cut across to the airfield and descend into the circuit pattern. It soon becomes apparent that the breeze is also blowing at Kalbarri Airport as the windsock seems to be almost at breaking point, although thankfully it is almost parallel in direction to the runway.

Even so, as I make the final turn to make my approach to land there is a significant cross-wind component to this gusty wind. I work hard to control the Jabiru with my right hand on the yoke, doing my best to maintain some semblance of a constant approach speed and flight path with the throttle in my left. A gust rolls me without warning and I quickly roll the wings back to level flight. It's an exciting ride and at times the speed washes off suddenly, leaving the Jabiru hanging in the air, void of energy, until I can offer her a dose of airspeed to carry on. All the while I am completely prepared to abandon the landing if it gets too hairy, and I have enough fuel and daylight to fly to Geraldton, a hundred miles away, if need be. But for the moment, it is difficult, not dangerous.

The headwind means that it is a slow ride down to the runway where a Fokker 50 airliner is waiting to depart. I gather that I am the entertainment for the passengers and crew as they watch the mighty little Jabiru do battle with the conditions. Finally, the runway is within inches of the wheels and I ease in the rudder and lower one wing to align the aeroplane with the runway. Right in front of the critical audience of the Fokker's crew, I touch down, slow down and turn around. Phew!

My relief is echoed by the airliner's pilot who transmits "I'm glad that was you!" as he enters the runway and waits for me to get out of their way. I waste no time in doing so, and as they roar into the sky I swing the Jabiru into a small windbreak provided by some thick undergrowth, and shut down the engine. I have been in the air for seven hours and 55 minutes of extraordinary flying, but now it's time to call it a day.

I climb out and push the Jabiru's tail well back towards the foliage before lashing her down very securely to a pair of concrete blocks. As I unload my gear I share a few insights with a reporter from Kalbarri before my lift arrives, and I head off to Murchison Station for the night. The station owner, Calum, and his daughter sit in the front of the truck as I lean back on the seating in the rear in the company of a couple of fierce looking "pig dogs". Never a big fan of canines, these two dogs occasionally growl at each other as we bump along the dirt road, but thankfully seem uninterested in me.

Calum offers me an ice cold beer and although I have not consumed a single alcoholic drink on this trip so far, the frigid drops running down the side of the bottle are just too hard to resist at the conclusion of eight hours in the seat. As I drink the amber fluid I can feel the cooling effect immediately and lean my head back in a thoroughly relaxed state, chatting with Calum as we drive on.

When we enter Murchison Station there is a mix of buildings, the historic homestead, beautiful climbing plants and even rusting military vehicles, including a tank. After nights in hotel rooms and cabins, the intimate surrounds of this historic, working station are just what I need. The station has been active for over 150 years and I can't wait to stow my gear and absorb the history.

Calum shows me to my lodgings; they are refurbished shearers' quarters that were built by convicts in 1860. There are some telltale signs of their convict builders even today. The large door-bolt is only lockable from the outside, while the lone small window would not allow a man to escape. Inside, the walls have been rendered, but one small section has been framed and preserved to show its original form. The ceiling is low, but the air is cool by virtue of the thick stone walls. This is great!

As the sun is getting low, Calum suggests that we head straight out to the place that motivated me to stay at Murchison Station in the first place. I jump into a four-wheel drive and we trek through the scrub to a small clearing littered with headstones. A number of the headstones dated back to the founding days of the station, but it is two old headstones and a low fence that catch my eye.

They are of Bob Fawcett and Eric Broad. They were contemporaries of Sir Charles Kingsford Smith and had been killed in 1921 when their Bristol Tourer biplane stalled while circling above a fellow aircraft that had been forced down with mechanical issues. The flight had been the first scheduled air service in Australia, a freight run, but was cut short in the wake of the tragedy. The outcome was that the service was placed on hold until sufficient emergency landing fields could be constructed throughout the Western Australian outback. During that time, QANTAS grew from strength to strength on the other side of the country and the rest is history.

Now I stand at this remote, forgotten graveside, so significant to our aviation history, and pay my respects to these lost aviators. As I do so, Calum points just over the way to where the aircraft tragically struck the ground. The wind and the isolation only add to the solemnity of the site and I am deeply moved.

I return to my shearers' quarters and sit on the verandah, chatting with some young backpackers who are working their keep at Murchison. Having a warm shower is like a shot in the arm and that night I share a meal with my hosts at the homestead and learn more of the history. It is a tremendous feast of chicken and vegetables that I consume at a savage pace. Seated around a table on the lawn under the stars, stories change hands and Calum relates that when he first arrived there were some ageing ladies who still recalled with a smile when "Smithy" came to Murchison.

Once again, generosity comes to the fore and Calum and his wife Belinda insist that my night's stay is "on the house" as their contribution to the work of the Royal Flying Doctor Service. Once again I am embarrassed, grateful and in admiration of outback fellowship. We enjoy dessert and a couple more tales and the entire occasion feels more like old friends catching up than a host-guest-worker relationship. This is Australia at its egalitarian best.

I bid one and all goodnight and make my way to my digs by torchlight. There is no Internet connection, so it is a night without news reports, interviews, blogs or updates. I stop to fill a jug of water in the kitchen where a harmless python resides in the drawer, before walking to my room and unlatching the convict bolt to enter. My torch beam reveals a coating of huge moths on the corrugated ceiling and I resolve to leave them alone if they'll reciprocate the favour. In minutes I am horizontal and ready to sleep in the darkest room one can imagine. It's blissful.

I roll over to set the alarm on my phone with some very soft music to play. I am totally relaxed. I can still hear the wind outside and I think of my Dad and of the lost aviators' graves, miles from home. So much has happened since the sun rose in Broome. The music is still playing gently as I am lost to the world for the night.

***

28

PEOPLE POWER

In 10 days I had literally travelled from Waikiki Beach to Werribee, Australia. I had crawled over two seat trainers and World War Two warbirds, bizjets and bombers. On the few days in between, the first *50 Tales of Flight* was released as an eBook, and then the controlled chaos of an international air show consumed my attention. Now I could stop to draw breath.

As always, so many stories were gathered and now they were bouncing around in my head, waiting to be released onto the page. However, if I was to draw a common thread between the diverse locations and range of aviation hardware I'd recently experienced, it would undoubtedly be the people. Faces that I had never seen before, and many I would most likely never see again. All sharing a common interest in aviation, they had walked into my path and impacted my life in a variety of ways.

First, there was Pearl Harbour. Crowds shuffled to and fro between museums and monuments wearing audio-tour headsets, locking out the sounds of the real world. And while the words spoken were informative, they could tend to consume one's focus, directed by the narrator more than the broader picture. Amongst this audio input, my wife wandered across to an elderly gentleman sitting quietly in the corner of a hangar behind a small table. Out of the way, he wore a Pearl Harbour golf shirt, with drawings of the museum's grand plan hanging on the wall. Alone and looking a little awkward, my wife engaged him in conversation and the warmth began to flow in his words.

He told her he was a veteran of the attack on Pearl Harbour in 1941. As a young man he had been at work on a flying boat, only metres away from where we now stood. Overlooked by the passing crowd, he spoke of the sounds and the chaos of the day. He also spoke about his love of the Catalina and flying light aircraft in later life. This man was living history and shared his story with us generously as the tour groups were caught up taking photos with their iPhones or trying on baseball caps. My wife had seen beyond that and we both reaped the rewards.

Fast forward a week and the busy scene that is an international air show in Melbourne, Australia. Held every two years, it draws global players on the trade days and massive crowds on the weekend. There is everything from heavy military hardware to ultra-lights. Every piece of hardware you could imagine is showcased in either the skies above, or in one of the mammoth exhibition halls. It can be hectic, to say the least, with so much to see and always a limited timeframe to do it in. Yet, once again, there was merit in taking the road a little less travelled and pausing to speak with the people.

I spent a good deal of time in the exhibition hall, manning the stand for one of the magazines that I write for. Always enjoyable, what was particularly special was the opportunity to meet the people who had read my words in the magazines, on the Internet or in my books. Putting faces to the people who take the time to read what I write. I was fascinated at the interest in stories from many deadlines ago and the enthusiasm exuded by these good folks. At this point, the hours of early morning typing seemed very worthwhile. Rather than a signal sent out into the void, the readers provided the echo to remind me that something was actually being said. And I know it wasn't just me, every writer at the magazine enjoyed the buzz of speaking with the readers.

On the flight-line, fighter pilots patiently answered the questions of kids and grandparents backed up just a few inches more for that perfect photograph. As jets roared vertically, arms stretched upwards with flattened palms, blocking out the sun in a form of air show salute. Excitement was everywhere. It may have been generated by the aircraft, but it came to life through the people. The hum of the crowd and the shared looks and nods as the F-22 Raptor manoeuvred aggressively, or a sailplane gracefully looped at dusk.

Aircraft can roar, crackle and whistle, but oohs, aahs and laughter are solely human traits. The air show also unveiled the faceless performers who are usually trapped beneath their canopies and helmets. Chatting with the crowds, shaking hands and signing books, like the crowd, they too are people. The air show seemed to bring out the best machinery and the best in people. The mood was as high as the sky that was filled with increasing frequency.

I decided to wander, take a moment and ponder the past. I entered the Air Force museum's exhibition, complete with a rag-and-tube machine and relics from an era now long gone. On the wall, a massive TV screen cycled through ancient black-and-white images. One after the other, photos of biplanes appeared with their struts and open cockpits, but once again it was the faces; the people. The pilots were young men on the edge of aviation's dawn, grinning from beneath goggles and oil-splattered mechanics standing proudly beside their machines. Where did their lives take them? Did they survive the wars? What was it like up there? My unanswered questions all seemed to stem from the people and their feelings, rather than the fascinating aircraft I was looking at.

Often, aviation can draw the attention with its marvels of technology. Its impressive record over the last hundred years of going farther and faster captures the imagination. However, we still need to pause and listen to the people, as difficult as that is to the background of roaring jets. Stop and take in the words of that war veteran who witnessed Pearl Harbour, or the child with a question about some great steel bird. For it is the human condition that provides the really awesome performance.

As I pondered this thought, the scream of a jet overhead suggested that perhaps I should join the mass of people once again. Still the screen flicked over, image after image. Face after face. Story after story. And then there was one that I recognised, sitting in the cockpit of a Mustang with engineers standing on either wing, the engine roaring and the propeller's slipstream seemingly blowing them away as they gripped the cockpit's frame. This face too was long gone; a life well lived. All those years ago, captured in black and white, a grin on his young face. It was my Dad.

***

29

48 Years in 3,000 Feet

Another day is drawing to a close like so many more before. The city looms ahead with its skyscrapers and bridges jutting above the horizon long before homes and highways can be discerned from the surrounding contours. All is ready on the flight deck and the passengers are strapped in safe and sound behind the bullet-proof door that our unfriendly times have fitted to my aircraft.

The needle on my electronic flight instrument creeps slowly down the screen, indicating that the time is approaching when I leave the comfort of level flight at 3,000 feet and begin my descent towards the black asphalt gateway of home with its stripes and cryptic numbers. One more "3 degree slope", once again edging 300 feet down for every mile closer and all the while slowing this finned-dart to a speed where it can safely reunite with the earth. It's a busy time, but one that never gets old.

"Flaps One." I call it and the other pilot reaches down and moves the lever between us, commanding the flaps to begin their journey along the leading edges of our wings. Curling into the airflow, the sheets of alloy allow us to fly this gravity-defying machine safely at speeds where it would fall without them. With the thrust levers sitting back against their stops at "idle" the engine noise is minimal and the smooth air offers a silky ride as we decelerate.

I look ahead and the city is a little larger now. Snaking through its heart is a river flowing down from the mountains to the sea via the beauty of Sydney Harbour. Within its banks courses water that began amongst the gum tress, but matures at the steps of an Opera House and beneath the steel arch that spans the harbour's shores.

For me that's where it all began; closer to the gums than the city lights. On the banks of that river in a small hospital in 1964 my mother gave me life in the midst of a thunderstorm at eight in the morning. Were the gods trying to tell her something? The needle on the instrument sits centrally and now announces that it is time to slide down the slippery slope.

"Flaps Five". The flaps bite the air just a little more; just a nip. And the speed slows in smooth response. We are still travelling at 350 km/h but the world below still seems to be in no particular hurry. I spy the runway in the distance, but there is still a good deal of time til we touch down.

As the river draws closer, its banks yield more of its character and more of my life. The towering statues atop the towering sandstone halls in front of which I stood bloodied, muddied and proud to wear the colours of my school. A mere boy with my mates by my side, goalposts ahead of me and wanting for nothing more in the world.

And the Olympic Stadium where I watched champions score their goals as our country showed the world its very best face and the new millennium arrived without a single computer crashing. What a beautiful view...what a beautiful town.

"Gear Down". The rumble moves through my seat as the wheels leave their home in the wings for one of their two moments of fame that come and go with every flight. The noise of the air moving past this new obstacle increases and "dangling the Dunlops" eases the speed back towards 280 km/h.

The red brick blocks of the Ambulance Academy stand out against the bright green grounds that surround it and lead to the water's edge. It was there that I learned the name of every human bone and the skills needed to piece a broken body back together. Yet even with all of the textbooks and knowledge, no classroom could ever prepare a 19-year-old for that first wet, dark night and the remnants of a man ejected through the window of his car, now lifeless. One eye open and staring, still caught off guard by the final card fate had dealt him.

"Flaps 15". I move another lever to arm the speedbrakes to pounce when the wheels eventually touch the ground. For the moment, there is a significant chomp of the airflow as the flaps to the rear of the wing move their mass into the path of the molecules. The nose lowers a touch and the speed slips back even further towards its final goal. The detail of the city is now becoming very much clearer and with that intimacy the sense of speed becomes more obvious.

Beyond the river is our first home as a couple. A small, century-old cottage with a corrugated roof, walls as thick as a castle's. It was over that threshold that I carried my gorgeous wife 15 years ago, and within those walls that I first learned how irrelevant my life is without her.

"Flaps 30". The last of the flaps extend to complete the re-formed wing and I move the speed selector for the last time back to the speed at which we will meet the runway; 130 knots. We complete the checklists and all is well with the aeroplane and our procedures as the thrust levers stabilise at a comfortable power-setting.

The runway looms large, but right beneath my nose is my school. Those clear summer days and the crack of the new red ball on the cricket bat. A treasure trove of memories, but the place where I was banned from sitting beside the window in class, so distracted was I by the jets and propellers buzzing overhead. It's funny how things turn out; I'm still looking out the window.

Runway One-Six-Right sits before me as the control tower clears us to land. This paddock of planes where I first flew in a tiny two-seater with my Dad beside me and where I am now entrusted with hundreds behind me. Orange stars, red virgins and tiger stripes adorn the tails of new airlines where only my blue fins once parked, but that was another airline, another life. Now I live amongst the kangaroo tails and they have taken me around the world and back many times and offered me so many sights that I shall never forget. But for the moment, the airport perimeter fence comes and goes.

The speed is right and the power where I want it. Now it is time for science, art and luck to combine and turn this mass of metal from a flying miracle to an awkward land vehicle. I ease back on the controls and retard the throttles to idle as the jet continues its trajectory towards the point on which I have been so focussed. The computer's voice calls out the last remaining heights..."30 feet - 20 feet". And then I wait. Squeak or thump?

It's somewhere in between as the wheels meet the pavement and the speedbrakes rise to spoil the wings' shape and dump the lift that it is designed to produce. As a result, the weight of the aircraft sits firmly on the wheels and the automatic brakes kick in with an effectiveness that throws us a little forward in our harnesses. I extend the levers on the front of the throttles and the engines roar into reverse as the thrust is redirected forward. We slow down and we rumble until flight is but a memory and the passenger terminal calls.

And so another day draws to a close with the same wonder of the day before. The vantage point of the sky above can offer a view that is seemingly endless, or it can provide detail of the world that will never be seen from the footpath. If we let it, flight can also lay out our life before us. Individual milestones drawn together like pinpoints on a map of our own personal history, the places and, most importantly, the people. No two days of flight are ever the same and each time we leave the earth behind we may just be marking a new pinpoint on the map of our life.

The landscape may be sliding by at breakneck speed below us, but there is always time to remember and to make new memories. And sometimes, if you are truly lucky, you may just be able to fit 48 years into 3,000 feet.

***

30

FLYING WITH THE LORD OF THE RINGS

We who fly are so fortunate. Once, man was confined to the highest tree on the highest hilltop to gain the best vantage point. We who fly sit so much higher above the world with all manner of places to take in. Personally, I have seen volcanic lava flowing by night and the Eiffel Tower by day. I have felt the history of those who have gone before as I descended over the English Channel and watched the dancing green curtain of the Aurora Australis in the night sky as I made my way from Johannesburg to Sydney. Still, there is one sight that I see frequently from the skies that captures my breath every time. It is the fabled land of the *Lord of the Rings*.

Located on the south island of New Zealand, the township of Queenstown and its surrounding lands were chosen to become the fabled Middle Earth described by J.R.R. Tolkien in his series of tales. His books detail mystical lakes and towering terrain with lush forests and pastures wedged in between. From above it can easily be seen why this land was chosen for the film as mile after mile of dramatic scenery sweeps by.

Queenstown was also chosen as a pioneering airport in the development of Required Navigation Performance (RNP) instrument approaches. The high terrain surrounding the runway precluded the straight flightpath needed for the traditional

Instrument Landing System (ILS) and left only non-precision approaches with high minimum altitudes to guide inbound aircraft. This was less than ideal given the clouds that lurk amongst the peaks and snow that can fall in the freezing winters.

In contrast, the RNP approach doesn't call for a long, straight, final approach leg. Just as an ILS can be seen as a rigid, narrowing funnel leading to the runway's end, the RNP approach can be considered to be a flexible hose that can wind its way through the terrain until the very last stage of the approach. By virtue of this, the scenery on show on a clear day is both spectacular and close at hand.

Still out to sea, the nose lowers and the engines retard to idle for the descent. Ahead, towering snow-capped mountains span the horizon and in the distance Mount Cook's summit spears over 12,000 feet into the atmosphere. Beyond the aircraft's nose the deep green coastline meets the dark blue waters, but the union is not subtle. Wild winds over the Tasman Sea are whipping up white caps on the crests of the waves while jagged cuts in the rocky shore provide entrances to deep waterways, or "sounds".

It is a land carved by glaciers and these sounds boast dark depths within and skyscraper cliffs all around. Waterfalls tumble hundreds of feet into the ocean shallows below as sparse vegetation and mosses struggle to cling onto the sheer rock faces. At the far end of Milford Sound a small runway sits wedged between a wall of rock at one end and friendlier waters at the other. There is only one way in and one way out.

Either side of the flight deck, the coating of snow shines brilliantly in the daylight with ice-capped lakes filling the craters at their peaks. A strong tailwind of 60 knots still pushes the Boeing along as it descends and the mountains momentarily give way to the upper reaches of the massive Lake Wakatipu. Despite the winds aloft, eerily lake is eerily picture-perfect and calm with the landscape reflecting in its glassy surface. The hamlet of Glenorchy provides the only signs of life in Middle Earth and soon the ski fields and peaks return.

Flaps are now extended from the swept silver wings to assist in slowing the jet down in readiness for landing. The runway now sits parallel and well below, but there are still a good many miles to weave before it is time to land. As the winds meet the landscape in an unforgiving exchange, the turbulence buffets the aeroplane and both pilots strain against their seatbelts with each jab. To the left, the racetrack at a cold-weather car-testing facility carves through the snow like an errant worm as the aircraft peels away to the right.

It is not "peak season" and skiing is not in full swing, although the helicopters that ferry the skiers still dart about at low level. Queenstown Airport is now dead ahead in the distance at the end of a meandering valley which is further defined by the watercourse that runs through it. As the wheels are lowered, cars are parked and people wave from a lookout that is almost level with the cockpit and not too far away. Below, the river passes beneath Bungy Bridge where the first person decided to give birth to a sport by leaping from its railings with rubber cords tied to their ankles.

The snow has now given way to the green rolling fields and signs of civilisation. To the left the face and peaks of "The Remarkables" tower above the Boeing, as if it were but an insect in their midst, while to the right are homes and towns within a naturally formed, bowl-like basin. With only minutes until landing, and all of the checklists complete, the RNP approach still jinks the aircraft gently along the best path, clear of the terrain.

One more green tree-topped knoll and one more slewing jet-boat below and the aircraft is finally aligned above the runway at only a few hundred feet. The runway is short by international airport standards, but adequate for the smaller 737s and Airbus A320s that share the airspace with a wealth of general aviation aircraft. The wheels touch, the speedbrake rises from its detent and the reverse thrust is deployed without delay. Soon the aircraft is parked and another spectacular sector is over.

Queenstown is a magical place that is even more dramatic when viewed from above. There are so many places across our planet that offer so much from the bird's-eye view that we are so fortunate to share. Whether we are whistling across the landscape in a jet, or dawdling past in a biplane, the world's majesty is on show for us in such a special way. It is in our own backyard, wherever we are, and we all have the opportunity to travel to our own Middle Earth.

***

Picture Perfect. Queenstown, New Zealand.

Seismic over Sydney. The Airbus A380 Formation.
(Image:'Australian Aviation')

31

FLYING A GIANT

Volunteering to climb aboard a flight simulator under the watchful eyes of two senior training captains on a rostered day off is not generally regarded as "normal" behaviour for a commercial pilot. However, when the aircraft involved is the newly arrived Airbus A380 and one's licence renewal isn't on the line, this is a case of pleasure rather than pain. And the pleasure began from the moment Check Captains Andrew and Rob opened the door to the massive flight deck of the A380 simulator. This sense of space is further enhanced by the wrap-around screens that offer a 200-degree view of the virtual world in the horizontal plane and 40 degrees vertically.

The side-stick control opens up the area immediately in front of the pilot and this space is utilised by a foldaway tray table and computer keyboard. To the side, the window frames extend quite low, much like on the Boeing 757, and offer a welcome addition to the peripheral visibility. The outlook belies the aeroplane's behemoth dimensions, and yet somehow there is not the sense of towering above the runway as from its double-deck compatriot, the 747.

Lined up on Sydney's Runway 16 Right for a 560 tonne takeoff weight, Rob enters the key data and the most striking factor is the relatively low speeds for such a large aeroplane at maximum weight. Spanning almost 80 metres, the huge surface area of the A380 wing employs new design concepts and manufacturing processes to ensure that the wing is as "clean" and efficient as possible. This efficiency translates not only into lower takeoff speeds, but compared to the 747-400 it uses 17 per cent less runway to get airborne. Cleared for takeoff, the thrust levers are brought up to initially stabilise power at 30 percent. Yes, per cent. These Rolls-Royce engines had, for the first time, dispensed with the aviation terminology of engine pressure ratios (EPRs) as a power setting and employed the metric equivalent. With power stabilised, the thrust levers are advanced through a series of detented "gates" that are characteristic of Airbus aircraft. Set at maximum power, the engines modulate to maintain the thrust with no corresponding movement of the thrust lever beyond its setting in the correct gate. Interesting.

Rumbling along the centreline, the A380 simulator provides all of the sensory cues to reinforce that this aircraft is at its maximum weight. The time to reach flying speed is further lengthened by the strong philosophy of de-rated takeoffs that exist with the type; even at such high weights. The reasons for this are diverse and range from lower maintenance costs to a reduced airport noise footprint.

Only 10kt separates the go/no-go speed, or V1, and the speed at which I need to raise the nose, or rotate. I tentatively pitch the aircraft towards 12 degrees nose up, note a positive rate of climb and call for the wheels to be raised. It becomes immediately apparent that Rob and Andrew are right on the money in cautioning me against over-controlling. The aircraft requires only small inputs and a degree of anticipation that you would expect of an aircraft of this size and weight. Now is an appropriate time to confess to having had some trepidation about the side-stick. Having only known the Boeing yoke during my 14 years in airlines, my sidestick record was not good. One attempt at a friend's Microsoft Flight Simulator after a Christmas barbeque that went rather badly and resulted in me wanting to bend the stick past the limits of its gimbals.

Fortunately, the real thing is tremendously intuitive and easy to fly.

Quite simply, within minutes you develop a feel for the control inputs and the sense of ease in steering this enormous airliner. The fundamental challenge in adapting to the side-stick stemmed from the need to input only enough control to achieve the desired attitude and then *release it*. There is no need to hold the control input in through a manoeuvre, you simply set it and then relax the input to neutral. The A380 will automatically trim and hold that attitude until you input the sidestick again to set a new attitude. As Rob stated from the outset, you "adjust" this aircraft around the sky. Less is definitely more.

A key Airbus philosophy is its "Laws of Protection". A mantra to Airbus fly-by-wire crews, these laws incorporate a series of flight mechanisms that define the boundaries of the flight envelope and protect the crew from exceeding it in an unsafe manner. These protections are designed to prevent the aircraft being stalled, taken over-speed, over-banked or accelerated beyond the limiting speeds for flaps. The first example of this function occurred after takeoff when the normal act of flap retraction was ignored as the aircraft accelerated. On reaching 212 knots, without any pilot input, the flaps begin the process of retraction to protect themselves from the stresses of excessive airspeed. The progress of the retraction can be followed on a schematic display in front of the pilot.

With the flaps retracted, we climbed out over the suburbs and flew a series of general handling exercises. The intuitiveness of the side-stick was really beginning to settle in by this time. The ease was aided by a flight guidance system referred to as "The Bird" that indicates the aircraft's trajectory, independent of body angle. If you place The Bird on the horizon bar, you will maintain level flight with a minimum of effort. In the turn, there is no need to hold in back pressure or trim the A380 until the bank angle reaches 33 degrees. Beyond this angle, back pressure is required to be held in as a reminder to the pilot that he is beginning to enter a phase of flight beyond the everyday boundaries. At 67-degrees of bank, the aircraft refuses the request to bank any further, regardless of control inputs.

At both ends of the speed envelope, the A380 also draws a line in the sand. Maintaining level flight, the thrust levers were closed and the aircraft decelerated towards its lowest safe-flying speed, through the amber warning bars on the speed tape towards the red indicator of the stall speed. With the thrust levers still retarded to the stops, the auto-protection is initiated and the engines spool up to maximum thrust and will not permit you to stall the aircraft. Again the thrust levers have not moved. If you had the speedbrakes extended, the system would have retracted these also. Once the aircraft senses the side-stick commanding an angle of attack below the angle at which the wing will stall, the pilot regains control of the aircraft. It all seems to straightforward.

Similarly, at the high-speed end of the regime with thrust on and diving towards the red "barber's pole" of overspeed territory, the system allows a momentary overshoot into this realm before acting. Again, independent of thrust lever and side-stick position, the aircraft reduces thrust and pitches its nose up to return the A380 to a safe operating speed until the pilot's actions once again indicate that he is heading in the right direction. In the early days of Airbus, these Laws of Protection had been an area of some confusion for crews.

Two decades have now passed and the logic they employ is better understood. As a first-timer I was suitably impressed, no more so than when I was encouraged to stall the aircraft on final approach in the landing configuration with the thrust levers closed and full aft and roll input. We should have fallen out of the sky, but despite my best efforts the A380 powered up, limited my bank angle and carefully set the pitch attitude to recover. I entered a climbing spiral to safety on short final and the rooftops below gradually became more distant. Did it feel natural? No. Was it amazing? Absolutely!

Yet I can't escape the belief that no system ever relieves the crew of their fundamental responsibility to fly the aeroplane and respect that "Power + Attitude = Performance".

With the simulator visual display repositioned at Sydney, we set about testing the A380's performance and handling with an engine failure on takeoff at V1 and the subsequent management of the event. As Rob called "V1", the telltale swing indicated that one of the Rolls-Royce Trent engines had failed. The rudder input to keep straight was minimal and when Rob called "rotate", the nose was easily pitched to a slightly lower-than-normal 10 degrees up and the climb away commenced at a very acceptable rate. The engine failure turned out to be an outboard engine, which naturally induces a greater yawing moment, or "swing", yet only moderate control input was required to keep the aeroplane flying straight ahead by virtue of the large rudder on the A380's enormous fin. The input needed for a failure of an inboard engine must be almost negligible, though this wasn't experienced on the day.

At a safe altitude and with the autopilot engaged, we set about addressing the engine failure. The Electronic Centralised Aircraft Monitoring (ECAM) pops up onto the central screens automatically in the event of a non-normal situation in conjunction with the appropriate system display. It leads the crew through the required checklists and actions in a very user-friendly manner as they set about resolving any failure that may occur – in our case the engine failure. It doesn't replace the pilot's need to remain unrushed and manage the situation, but what it does offer is the best available information to support the process in a very logical format. With the problem addressed, we restarted the engine and made our approach to land back at Sydney. We took in some mandatory sightseeing over the harbour city and the visuals are just as you'd expect from a simulator of this generation, with the landscape not only accurately portrayed, but casting shadows as well.

The approach itself was like much of the flight – very stable and controlled with minimal pilot input. In fact, it all seemed to evolve very slowly as, once again, the speeds for this vast aircraft are relatively low. As the runway loomed large in the window and the radar altimeter started to call out my height, I began to check the descent at about 40 feet as briefed by Rob. Looking ahead, the aircraft settled onto the runway with a minimum of fuss and I reached down to deploy reverse thrust. Interestingly, by virtue of the lower speeds and braking system, the A380 only possesses reversers on the inboard engines. Even so, we pulled up after a surprisingly short ground roll. The fun had come to an end.

The arrival of the Airbus A380 in our skies created a buzz and people still crane their necks to catch a glimpse of the giant overhead. I consider myself very fortunate to have had the opportunity to experience a flight in the simulator of this amazing aircraft. Its flight characteristics seem to ooze simplicity and are ably supported by its systems and redundancies. Even the side-stick is no longer a spectre to this old Boeing pilot. It is intuitive, simple and all about subtlety. For me there is absolutely no longer any temptation to bend this side-stick past the limit of its gimbals.

***

32

SEISMIC IN THE SKY

As necks craned and eyes were cast skyward in Sydney, Australia, the sight of two Airbus A380s in formation overhead was something to behold. Yet even for a flight that was little more than a hop for the long-haul airliners, a great deal of preparation, planning and training had been called for. Only then could these giants take to the skies in each other's company.

The flypast was initially planned in secret, with the first simulator sessions flown in the wee hours to design a flight profile and define what training would be needed. This was the task of First Officer Jim Eaglen, a former RAAF fighter pilot with experience on Mirages, Tornados and Hornets. Along with First Officer Andrew Eastaway, through the course of 10 four-hour sessions in the simulator, they crafted a plan, at which time Captain Peter Barry, also ex-RAAF, was brought into the loop. Their task now was to compile training plans and briefing packages, as well as flying another three sessions in the A380 simulator to confirm that the flight profile was just right.

At this point the plan started to emerge, with Emirates pilots flying in the simulator with their QANTAS compatriots and then demonstrating the flight profile to the Civil Aviation Safety Authority (CASA) and their respective company Chief Pilots. Additional QANTAS crew were chosen to fly the sortie with former RAAF fighter combat instructor (FCI) Sean Trestrail as "pilot flying" and Second Officer Mark Cameron, bringing the total crew complement to four, with Captain Barry joining the Emirates crew to provide local knowledge. In addition to Captain Barry, the Emirates A380 had Captain Abbas Shaban at the helm with former Belgian Air Force F-16 pilot, Captain Peter De Roeck and South African Mirage pilot, First Officer Patrick Flynn.

The Emirates crews flew additional sessions in their own simulator to further consolidate the requirements of the task. In all, 22 simulator sessions were flown in preparation, but the training did not stop there. There were written briefings to absorb, and formal whiteboard briefings to attend before and after each simulator session. Captain Barry, a former RAAF flying instructor (QFI), was the man behind producing these briefings.

Second Officer Mark Cameron was kept busy attending to many of the administrative and regulatory issues. As one can imagine, proposing to fly two aviation behemoths over Sydney Harbour requires a number of formal issues to be negotiated. A comprehensive risk analysis of the sortie was conducted and measures were put in place accordingly. Pivotal was thorough preflight training and the selection of experienced crews with a comprehensive background in formation flying. Captain Barry wrote yet another very comprehensive brief, this time for CASA, and they in turn observed the simulator training. A healthy exchange of information followed and a number of approvals were ultimately issued to fly over a public gathering, in formation. Approvals were also required from the UAE General Civil Aviation Authority (GCAA).

With the "green light" from the regulator, Jim Eaglen and Mark Cameron then liaised with Sydney Air Traffic Control to obtain the appropriate clearances. Once again, a number of scenarios needed to be covered in preparation for the variables that could arise on Easter

Sunday, when the flight was scheduled to take place. The runway configuration at Sydney Airport, traffic management, airspace clearances and potential weather issues were just some of the topics addressed. These also had to be considered in the context of the manoeuvrability of an Airbus A380 formation.

After five weeks of intensive preparation, the formation flight was finally set to take place. The QANTAS A380 VH-OQJ carried the callsign of "QANTAS 6600", while the Emirates crew flew A6-EDY under the banner of "Emirates 8388". Together, their formation was named "Seismic". This name hailed from a reference in a speech by Emirates Airline President Tim Clark who described the two airlines partnership as a "seismic shift in aviation".

After a hundred hours of simulator training, the 45-minute flight was now underway. With only the operating crew aboard each aeroplane, they lifted off at a "lightweight" 330,000 kg, well below their maximum takeoff weight of 569,000kg. Formed up, the two giant airliners entered Sydney Harbour from the east, before flying a reversal procedure and passing over Sydney from west to east and departing. On the ground, thousands of Sydneysiders stopped and lifted their eyes to see an unprecedented sight over their beautiful harbour. In the air, the crews set about executing the flight in the same professional manner in which they had trained so thoroughly.

The scene above was breathtaking as the two giants of the skies sat shoulder to shoulder in close company, casting a unique shadow over the cityscape. Fingers pointed skyward as the massive Airbuses wheeled about the sky in a style that is more familiar to jet fighter pairs than four-engined airliners. The cameras of professionals and amateurs alike clicked at a rapid rate to capture this rare moment and soon the world would share them.

By the time the A380s had landed, press releases and photographs of the event were popping up all over the Internet. It was an instantaneous response to a 10-minute flypast of Sydney Harbour that was actually many weeks and hours in the making. The smooth, uneventful nature of the flight belied the effort that lay behind it, as is so often the case in aviation.

"Seismic" had drawn together pilots from two airlines, of multiple nationalities with military backgrounds from around the globe. They had flown in simulators in Sydney and Dubai and yet shared a single stream of training to build a tight, efficient formation. The team had satisfied everyone from CASA to their own chief pilots that the exercise could be flown safely in Sydney's skies. And when the day came, that's exactly what they did.

In the modern airline era there is often little latitude for operations beyond the norm. When such an opportunity as the A380 formation does arise, it calls for an extensive investment of time, resources and dedication on behalf of all involved. Only when such a level of professionalism is displayed can very special moments be created in the sky. And only then does the opportunity exist to create a flight that is truly seismic.

***

33

A Classic Farewell

It could have been just another departure had it not been for the fire trucks spraying their watery salute. Just another capital city shuttle run, another day at the office. In fact, as the Boeing 737-400 spooled up to taxi under its own thrust, it was actually powering towards the end of an era. The 737 "Classic" was saying farewell to Australian skies.

The term "classic" is bandied about a good deal these days. Like "legend" and "awesome", the true meaning has been dulled by frequency of use. In the airliner world, the term has actually retained its original meaning in defining something of lasting worth or possessing a timeless quality. For the Boeing 737, the "Classic" was most readily identified by round analogue dials on the flight deck and an absence of blended winglets on its wing tips.

The first 737-100 flew in 1964 and little changed with the jet's appearance until the pencil-like Pratt and Whitney JT8D engines were replaced by the flat-bottomed cowlings of the high-bypass CFM-56 engines in the early 1980s. This change in powerplant gave birth to a larger range of aircraft, designated as the -300/-400/-500 series. In later years, these were the aircraft labelled as the "Classics".

The emergence of Airbus saw the birth of the 737's 'Next Generation' in the form of the -600/-700/-700 series. Towering winglets on some models, a more efficient wing, GPS navigation and an almost-fully "glass" flight deck transformed the aircraft in many ways. Still, much of the 1960s heritage could be found in areas like the flight deck's overhead panel, even if the systems behind the switches had changed. For those who flew her, the Classic still had a special place as technology raced on.

My personal relationship started with the Classic 20 years ago. At my airline interview, I had given the three-holer 727 as my first preference, but training on that fleet was winding down. My disappointment was short-lived as the 737-300 was still a big step up from the Barons and Chieftains that I had been bashing around the outback in.

It was my first simulator-supported type endorsement and my first aircraft with a functioning electric trim and autopilot. Those "accessories" hadn't rated highly in previous times. There was a truckload of manuals to study and an enthralling slideshow known as "Spiritus" in which a monotone voice stepped you through every operating system of the Boeing 737. At the core was a need to truly understand the systems of the aircraft, and this knowledge was questioned by all and sundry at every opportunity.

That being said, the Classic was a wonderful aeroplane in which to learn aircraft systems by the 1990s. It was a blend of old-world analogue with a touch of the new age. The primary flight and navigation displays were two "glass" or EFIS screens, one atop the other, and a flight management computer that allowed data entry and calculations to be performed through control display units, or CDUs, with green-lettered displays reminiscent of early digital watches.

Still, systems like the hydraulics and pressurisation were still of Boeing's tried and tested form. "Bleeds Off" takeoffs were common at heavy weights to squeeze out maximum performance, and this led to an intimate understanding of the auxiliary power unit (APU), air systems and the maze of ducting that tied them together. Similarly, there were means of "unloading" the APU at engine start on a hot day by deselecting a range of services, including the electric hydraulic pumps.

Like the Bleeds Off takeoff, these were drills that were committed to memory and founded on sound systems-knowledge. After simulator and ground school, 'Base Training' introduced the new pilot to the real aeroplane without passengers and even "engine out" circuits were flown about the runway at a secondary airport, away from the hustle and bustle. Today, base training has disappeared, the aircraft systems are simpler and checklists are the norm, but for a rookie, the 737 Classic taught me well.

For those who have flown the old and new 737s, few will argue that the Classic possessed better handling characteristics from a pilot's point of view. It sat comfortably above its optimum altitude in the cruise. The Classic was a great aircraft to land and rode gusty conditions on final approach with a steady hand. The -300 in particular had a sporty feel and the -400 wasn't far behind. However, it must be remembered that these were also times when breaking off a distance measuring equipment (DME) arrival and circling visually to a runway was commonplace. Handling was pivotal on dark, wet nights when the only real guidance cues were an altimeter, clock and a blurry line of runway lights out the side window.

Today, a visual circuit is rarely flown in a 737 and circling has been confined to the annals of history. Complex arrivals and approaches guide the aeroplane along computer-programmed tracks under the steady hand of the autopilot in most instances. As wonderful as the "old days" were from a pilot's perspective, hand-flying is not so common these days and the change is for the better in most cases. Operations are safer and more predictable, but we mustn't lose those handling skills altogether either.

This change in philosophy and growth in technology was ultimately what saw the Classic's days becoming numbered. There was no GPS fitted and its navigation system was guided by an inertial reference system (IRS) that required "updates" from ground-based aids. This meant that the navigation display could "drift" and the map that was portrayed didn't reflect the real world.

This shortcoming was particularly prevalent in the early days before flight management computer (FMC) technology caught up. It built up a healthy distrust and it only took one DME arrival into Cairns to see that the runway wasn't sitting quite where the map display suggested. The worst drift I ever saw personally was 12 nautical miles on a remote sector, although the map quickly righted itself as we flew into range of the VOR navigation aid. Despite the seemingly confusing conflict of information, one learnt that raw data was king and it was constantly referred to and tracked by. VOR radials, DME distances and non-directional-beacon (NDB) bearings were the trusted source of information and the map was nice to have when it was updated; but it was never entirely trusted. It must also be remembered that at the time, these systems were still significant improvements on what had gone before.

Time marched on and the clever folks in white coats rectified these issues and the Classic moved with the times. However, there were little idiosyncrasies that gave the aircraft character to those that flew her. Idiosyncrasies that will probably bring smiles to faces for many years to come.

On hot days, the air conditioning packs could work so hard that they started to spit small flakes of ice out of the vents at the pilot. There was the soft plastic drain hose that could get wedged into the window frame resulting in a constant squealing on takeoff that would only subside around 10,000 feet. The highly sensitive landing gear warning horn that continued to sound between flaps 1 and 10 and was cancelled by a tap to the "horn cut-out" near the thrust levers. The autothrottle switch that would disconnect on the ground during a flight control check. The alternate navigation control display unit (ANCDU) that provided a basic "back-up" navigation guidance system; rarely used, but an interesting exercise nonetheless.

As much as we loved the Classic, the introduction of the Next Generation Boeing 737 in Australia was both wise and warranted. The growth of GPS navigation and required navigation approaches (RNP) were beyond the scope of the Classic and the new models came with enhanced performance, systems and cabin amenities.

It was easy to view the aircraft purely from a pilot's handling perspective, but in reality its time had come. It was still a safe, reliable workhorse but the world had changed. The -800 can fly faster, further and higher, and above more of the weather. The -800 and its systems are more straightforward and offer greater support to the crews. In the cabin, the entertainment systems on offer today just couldn't be found on a Classic. As RNP approaches became more prevalent, the absence of a GPS on board limited the arrivals that the Classic could fly. With safety determining that circling approaches were also a thing of the past for 737 for many operators, the minimas were raised and another option was removed. The Classic wasn't a dinosaur, but it was getting left behind.

Much of the -800s advancements are built upon the legacy of the Classic. From extended range twin operations (ETOPS) and improved EFIS displays, to the simplified pressurisation system, Boeing has grown upon the winning formula of the 737 and continues to do so as the 737 MAX looms on the horizon. Still, the Classic will remain in reliable service across the globe and in freight operations in Australia for some time to come.

All good things must come to an end and, personally, I am sad to see the Classic depart. I am grateful for what it taught me about airline flying across a broad range of ports both domestically and internationally. Calculating "points of no return" to Noumea or New Zealand as the weather at Norfolk Island deteriorated, and peeling off the bottom of the NDB approach at Ayers Rock as heavy rain hammered the red centre – there was very little the Classic could not do; it's just that the -800 can do it better.

The last QANTAS 737-400 has now been parked in the "boneyard" at Victorville in the United States and the fire trucks final salute is already a fading memory. For those that flew the Classic, the memory shall not fade so fast and the debt of gratitude for many miles of safe passage will always remain.

As an airliner, it underpinned domestic airline operations for three decades and still had the reach to fly across seas to nearby neighbours. As an aircraft it was a joy to fly. Thanks for the memories and thanks for the new generation of aircraft that you spawned. As the 737 continues to develop and reach new heights, now might be the time to pause for a moment and bid the Classic farewell.

***

34

The View from Above

We only gained this lofty perspective in recent times. You could say that, ever since we first climbed down from the trees, we've been seeking to climb back up them. Higher, to a better vantage point, to observe our surroundings, both beautiful and hostile. First there came extended glimpses from balloons and gliders, then powered flight offered freedoms that had previously only been dreamed of.

So now we sit perched between the hills and the heavens, looking down on the earth from all manner of heights. Still, rather than occupying some aerial throne – rulers of the sky, as it were – we remain guests in a foreign realm. A realm that can turn and bite, or disorient, in an instant, with a fury that only nature can summon.

And yet we routinely visit this world aloft as passenger or pilot and marvel at the sights below. Sunsets and scenery that change not merely with the seasons, but by the moment. Remote red deserts or deep green waves enchant in their own special way, while man-made structures remind us where we ultimately belong. Homes, factories, offices and stadiums all gather on river banks, harbours and rail lines. Humans congregating and growing as communities, great and small.

An entire town may seem little more than a gathering of dots from a great altitude, while a low-level coastal flight may seem to place the cockpit in the eyeline of that town's residents. Towering skyscrapers that catapult humankind into the skies without ever leaving the ground and the unmistakeable mosaic of suburbia's red roofs.

And then there are the ghost towns. Isolated pockets of crumbling walls and failing fence lines, gradually collapsing back into the land from where they once sprung. Built on the hopes and dreams of pioneers, they are now perishing in the despair of isolation. Miles upon miles from anywhere, these hardy souls established a life where only sparse vegetation and even less wildlife had previously dared to exist. Whether they toiled in the soil or dug deep into the earth in search of fortune, there small community was their world. Now their world is in ruins and awaiting the inevitable fate at the hands of time.

All these communities, great and small, are on display to those who fly. Spectacular cities and remote villages are there for those who climb up amongst the clouds. The vista from altitude is special and the speed of flight can offer the extremes of human habitation in a matter of hours, if not minutes. The air offers a lifeline not visible to the human eye. Not only the gun-barrel highway or the pot-holed outback track over which wheels rumble. But those fine threads joined by cleared patches of dirt and asphalt on the city limits or in a farmer's paddock.

There for the interested traveller, businessman and medical evacuation alike, these landing fields give wings to a land-locked species. In straight lines and over undulations we can launch into that three-dimensional world and fly as far as the fuel tanks, wallet and airspace limitations permit. Uninhibited by the conventional laws of human movement and in an ongoing joust with gravity, flight enables us to see so much more of our world than we could ever have imagined. And the geometry need not always be the efficiency of a straight line from A to B, but the unbridled fun of wandering in the sky and loitering for a longer look.

Still, it is important to not become totally lost in the moment. We are venturing where some angels fear to tread. Beside a towering cumulonimbus cloud, the largest aircraft looks like a gnat. Turbulence, wind and rain can transform the environment so quickly and toss those aloft about with ferocity. And what of those below?

Yes, we are also privileged to fly above their roofs. The homes and businesses whose inhabitants are going about their day at sea level, generally oblivious to our presence unless the noise of an aircraft engine causes them to crane their neck and look skywards. Some will occasionally mutter a curse as well, but that's okay. We understand that their difference in opinion and perspective does not detract from the care we must take as we transit their lives at a distance.

We must always endeavour to minimise our impact on their world. Whether that is in day-to-day flying, or in the event of an emergency. It's best not to cause them to crane their necks unless it is an act of curiosity or envy, for there are those on the ground who would like us all to stay on the ground. We should plan to give their denser gatherings a little wider berth and ourselves unpopulated options should we need to "put down" in a hurry.

Obviously, these options are not always available, but we should always make an effort. The ability to co-exist makes for a better world, and the fact that our community resides amongst the cumulus doesn't makes us exempt. We must play our part as fellow land-dwellers and respect the fact that the gift of flight comes with some caveats. Compared to the benefits, it is a small price to pay.

To rise into the sky and view the world as our forefathers never could is a modern marvel. They sought out the highest mountains to survey their world, now we survey those mountains from above. Just as they placed their footsteps carefully upon the rising slopes, we must make our way carefully through the skies. Only when we venture forth with a balance of wonder and respect can we truly draw out the magic of flight and the world about us. And only then can we truly appreciate the view from above.

***

35

HORNET'S NEST

RAAF Base Williamtown is the spiritual home of Australia's jet fighter force. At the front gate a large billboard welcomes you to the "Hornet's Nest" as a less-than-subtle reminder of the squadrons of FA-18 Hornets at the ready on the apron beyond the security gates and towering fences. As I step out of my measly 1.5 litre Toyota Corolla, the air is alive with the sound of afterburners and another pair of fighters takes to the sky. They are two very different worlds on either side of this fence.

I am met at the security gate by Squadron Leader Ray Simpson, a veteran of the second Gulf War and a current Fighter Combat Instructor (FCI). Highly experienced on the FA-18, Ray's current posting calls for him to develop and oversee training, tactics and procedures for Hornet pilots and FCIs both in the aircraft and on the ground in the RAAF's two Hornet simulators. Today, I am gaining some insight into the training of Australia's fighter pilots by means of a "flight" in one of these simulators.

A short distance from the impressive line of Hornets on the tarmac, a tall, nondescript building sits anonymously. Yet within its walls are housed two very advanced flight simulators, facilitating the training of the next generation of Hornet pilots and maintaining the standards of those already operational. Upstairs is the instructor's station and all manner of whirring computers with technicians on hand to upload flight profiles and missions as required. Today's flight profile will be a combination of air-to-air combat, a bombing run and laser bomb sortie before returning to the circuit.

The instructor's station comprises eight large screens, each offering a wealth of varied information ranging from the pilot's flight display, head-up-display (HUD), armament status and position overlaid onto a real-world presentation which aids greatly in situational awareness. There are also two cameras in the simulator cockpit that allow the instructor to monitor the pilot's eye-scan and control inputs. As I am soon to learn, anything that can aid the pilot's appreciation of where he is and where he will be very shortly is a marvellous asset. Ray points out the various screens and their broad range of features at an incredible rate that reflects the depth of knowledge needed to operate a Hornet. He also highlights the datalink system that allows information to be digitally transferred between the aircraft in flight. Fuel, armament and altitude and speed are just examples of the information that a "leader" can access in a moment. Furthermore, it significantly reduces the need for radio chatter, making communications less intensive in critical phases and instrument flight.

Ray and I descend the metal staircase, complete some further paperwork and enter the room housing the simulator. It differs greatly from the enclosed white boxes of civilian airline simulators, lurching on their insect-like hydraulic legs. The Hornet simulator sits low to the ground, requiring only a step or two up to enter it. It is also very open with the "visuals" wrapping right around the pilot, even to the extent that there is the projection of his twin-fins on a screen behind him.

This wrap-around setting is achieved by a series of angular screens radiating from a central pentagonal screen in front of the pilot. It all seems very futuristic, but still relatively simple at a distance. The reason is because this simulator does not possess any "motion", as it is not possible to engineer the gut-wrenching, blood-draining physical impact of an 8G turn. Those physical demands are provided by the aircraft or a centrifuge. At this point I would like to reinforce that my previous use of the word "simple" was accompanied by the words "relatively" and "at a distance".

Ray shows me the small kit bag and knee-pad that is his standard kit for both flight and simulator missions. On these charts and notepads are an immense amount of data relating to the equipage of the aircraft, the planned sortie, the airspace to be utilised, any limiting parameters, communications data, navigational charts, individual roles in air-to-air scenarios. The list seems endless and then I am further taken aback when Ray informs me that the greater majority of the content is S.O.P. or standard operating procedure. This material is committed to memory and executed by the pilots unless briefed otherwise It's an amazing amount of information and further reinforces why thorough briefings are particularly critical in this type of operation. By this stage my head is spinning and I haven't even strapped in.

The moment of truth is rapidly approaching and I take the two small steps up and the big one down into the Hornet simulator. My first impressions are of daunting complexity in every direction as I lower myself into the ejection seat and begin to adjust its position and my harnesses. Slowly, I begin to recognise certain components from their logical location and ergonomic design. Gear, flaps, throttles, communications, head-up-display. However, I soon also become aware that even many of the "conventional" controls have additional buttons or toggle switches on them to provide the pilot with various systems close at hand. There is also an array of emergency levers, hashed in yellow and black, such as the emergency release for ordinance.

Between my legs, the control column rises from the floor and has a swathe of switches, triggers and buttons atop its bulbous handgrip. This is known as Hands on Throttle and Stick or HOTAS. The switches are designed this way as they would be inaccessible if placed anywhere else when pulling high g-forces. This is a very solid component, serving numerous purposes, and once again the pilot needs to know every function by feel and by heart. I strongly suspect that a fighter aircraft is not the place to be looking down when the heat is on.

Ahead, three glass screens fill the flight panel and provide everything from weapons selection and radar detection of foe, to the grainy green real-time footage of the targeting pod that has a camera that tracks and designates a target to guide a weapon to its target. The lower central screen provides the "moving map" while above it sits communication units (Up Front Control), topped by a head-up-display. Landing gear lever, flaps and throttles file down the left-hand side of the cockpit, while the right is equally congested with a range of selectors. This is one intense workspace.

I'm now settled in the seat and Ray assists me with fitting one of the new-generation helmets. It is known as the Joint Helmet Mounted Cuing System or JHMCS, pronounced "JeHemicks" by the pilots. Some of this helmet's functionality is classified, so I am only able to see the most straightforward data that it offers. That being said, this helmet has its own Head-Up-Display projected onto the visor, allowing me to look in any direction and still receive critical flight information that is normally only available straight ahead. These helmets also possess the ability to target an enemy in the air or on the ground by looking at them and cuing weapons without necessarily pointing the aircraft straight at them.

It is an amazing piece of equipment that extends the rim of the helmet further forward of the pilot's forehead, giving it a distinctly different shape. I'm instructed to close one eye and look at the far end of the runway and depress the trigger in order to set the HUD to my personal setting. I am all out of excuses, so it's time to fly.

Ray is perched beside the cockpit and runs through the critical speeds. Reject 135 knots. Rotate 155 knots. Wheels off at 170 Knots. The speeds strike me as not too dissimilar to a Boeing 737 as I open the throttles and push through the gate to engage the afterburner. The speeds may be similar, but we achieve them *a lot quicker* in a Hornet.

Before I know it, I'm rotating to 8-degrees nose-up, raising the gear and retracting the flap. All clean, we pull up to 40 degrees and the vertical speed is showing 15,000 feet per minute as Williamtown and planet earth disappear behind me. This is incredible.

My eyes are hunting to get the information I need from the HUD as the symbology scrolls up and down and arrows point left and right. We fly a series of turns, climbs and descents and I am overwhelmed by the lightness of the controls. My airline heritage shows through as I endeavour to smoothly guide the Hornet and roll out of turns with gentle anticipation. Ray reminds me that this is a fighter jet and to put the aircraft where I want it. Roll it briskly towards the new heading and then roll out with equal vigour. I start to get the hang of it and the fun factor steps up another notch.

Ray assists me with the systems and weapons selection as we acquire two targets closing at high speed, head-on and destined to pass down our right-hand side. The green vector in the HUD points to the target and I visually acquire the screaming dot ahead. I aggressively roll the aircraft and pitch down towards the target, which is a lot easier to do when you aren't sustaining massive g-forces. I roll in behind the target who conveniently doesn't try to evade me and I squeeze the trigger before he erupts in a ball of flame.

We turn back towards the other target who is now well below us, and again we take chase. This time we select an air-to-air missile using the HOTAS and the selection is confirmed on the top-left screen, then I wait until I have the target in my sights. Again, this enemy plays the game for me as I send a missile spearing towards him and he meets his demise. At this point, there are no g-forces and it is a straightforward training exercise against a co-operative enemy, but I can still feel my adrenalin rising.

Next we fly north at altitude to a simulated remote city of streets, low buildings and a network of roads. We change to air-to-ground mode by pushing one button and go to that top-left screen again and select a bomb this time before pitching the Hornet 30-degrees nose-down, diving at speed towards the target. In the HUD, the time to target counts down before I pickle the red button and bug out off the coast while the explosion takes place behind me. Over the water I fly low level at over 600 knots and the "ground rush" is incredible and I wonder what it would be like for real.

I then turn back towards the city which is growing very quickly in the HUD ahead. On Ray's cue I break right, pitch up to 15 degrees before rolling back towards the target at 10-degrees nose-down. This manoeuvre is designed to take the defensive positions by surprise and keep them guessing, but I admit that it had a similar effect on me as I released the bombs, totally consumed by target fascination.

Our final task is to release a laser-guided bomb. With a small "mouse like" switch near the throttles, I move the cursor to target the building displayed in the familiar grainy green infra-red on the top-left screen. I am flying at 15,000 feet and once again the time to target counts down in the HUD. On the mark, I pickle the release and get out of there as fast as I can, but even as I do so, the grainy green image continues to track and film the target as it guides the weapon. Like a scene on CNN from the Gulf War, I watch the dot erupt on impact and the target is no more. It's an almost surreal moment interrupted as Ray checks my situational awareness by asking where I am now in relation to the target. It emphasises to me that the level of vigilance can never be relaxed in these situations.

I commented on a feeling of asymmetry in the controls and Ray explains that the ordnance has been deployed from one side of the Hornet causing this situation. He reaches across and jettisons the remaining weaponry and the aircraft seems to grow extra speed and again feels balanced. Now flying clean, we head back to Williamtown and join the circuit.

By this stage I am getting a better handle on the HUD symbology and a basic feel for the aeroplane which now responds a little differently without the external ordinance hanging from its wings. We fly a series of circuits, the first one fairly wide and the subsequent tighter and more true to life. Ray prompts me what speeds I am looking for and when to lower the gear and flap initially and I am tentatively gaining some confidence at flying this simulator.

Rounding the base turn it was a combination of flying the real-world picture outside the cockpit with one eye hunting the performance measures. The thrust vector is known as the "E bracket" and is designed to fly the jet at the required 8.1 degrees AoA designed for arrested carrier landings. The primary attitude instrument is in the centre of the HUD and is known as the velocity vector (a flight path vector). The aircraft touchdown point can be anticipated by placing it on the threshold. As the wheels approached the runway, the urge to over-flare the aeroplane needs to be resisted and it is flown onto the markers positively before advancing the throttles and taking off again. Simply put, it is a tremendous challenge that I am thoroughly enjoying, but unfortunately it must come to an end. The last landing we use the Hornet's naval origins to lower the tail-hook and catch the arrestor cable. We stop in a hurry, but I have to throw myself forward in the harness without motion.

We shut the Hornet down and I sit there for a moment. I contemplate what has just transpired, trying to take it all in. It's not easy, as I have a mix of an adrenalin dump blended with a real sense of perspective.

My first reaction when I have caught my breath is an even higher sense of respect for the men who fly these aircraft. My father was a fighter pilot in Korea and always understated what was involved. His photo now hangs on the wall at Williamtown, staring back at me from the 1950s. For a little over an hour I had a glimpse of that world. It is a world of flying an extremely high-performance aircraft in the most challenging manner and still having to manage a wealth of systems and priorities, all the while maintaining a high level of situational awareness and vigilance for threats both within and external.

I felt a degree of fatigue after a simulated session without any g-forces acting upon my body. One can only imagine the powers of concentration needed to potentially fly long distances to hostile territory, refuelling en route and then operating in a combat environment, before hauling all the way back home. The level of fitness, powers of concentration and ordered thought under pressure is as impressive as the performance of the Hornet itself.

It is no wonder that so many youngsters aspire to a fast-jet cockpit in the RAAF and I admit to wishing I was a few decades younger. To fly a modern fighter is a complex task where acute manipulative skills meet a maze of systems management beyond the sound barrier. It is the cutting edge of the aviation spectrum and those who operate there can be rightly proud of what they do. For me, tomorrow it is back to the flight deck, two pilots and straight and level. For the fighter pilots of RAAF Williamtown, it will be another day in the Hornet's Nest.

***

FA-18 Hornet Simulator. (Image: Tim Visser-'Blue Lens')

Another Seahawk takes to the Sky.

36

BENEATH THE RADAR

Encountering flight can take place in so many settings. It can occur in the cockpit, reclining in the passenger cabin or simply by casting one's eyes skyward. In my travels and writings, I am very fortunate to see aviation from a number of perspectives and encounter a range of fascinating people. One summer's day, I gained an insight into flight above the waves beneath the thumping rotors of a military helicopter. However, first I needed to study the inner-workings of the navy's Fleet Air Arm through an intense flight simulator session...

I sit as a silent observer as the scenario is set for yet another training mission in the flight simulator. In this instance, political tensions are high in the region and the United Nation's has called upon the Royal Australian Navy to provide a secure perimeter beyond the borders of the threatened countries. The Australian Task Group is all that stands in the way when a potential threat is detected in the waters to the north.

On the deck of HMAS Sydney, a lone S70B-2 "Seahawk" lifts from the pitching, rolling deck and heads towards the lurking menace beneath the waves. On board the helicopter a crew of three works as one to home in on the target which is continuing to track towards the Task Force. In the front-left seat the Tactical Officer, or "TACCO", liaises with the HMAS Sydney and directs the pilot into the hostile area where a series of sonar buoys are dropped in a specific pattern in an attempt to triangulate the position of the submarine.

The first buoy measures the temperature, solidity and pressure of the water and sets a base-line, while the subsequent "active" buoys look for the intruder. All the while, back in the cabin, the "Sensor Operator" scans his screen looking for the telltale acoustic signs of the submarine, and it's not long before he has a "hot" contact. The level of chatter increases amongst the crew and, in turn, with the bridge of the Sydney, where the ultimate decisions will be made. The TACCO plots a tighter course, while the "Senso" gleans more and more vital identifying information from the ragged lines on his gleaming green screen.

The target is identified as an enemy submarine and, in keeping with the rules of engagement, two warning drops are made, but there is no response from the aggressor. The order is given from the Sydney and an attack is made on the hostile submarine, halting it in its tracks. No sooner than the Seahawk has completed its mission than another surface target is detected further to the north.

The TACCO gives the pilot a course to steer as he heads off towards the new threat at a mere 200 feet above the waves. Meanwhile, the Senso is switching his priorities from acoustic sensing to visual acquisition using the Forward Looking Infra Red (FLIR) system mounted on the Seahawk's nose. Minutes later he sights the vessel on his screen and indentifies it as enemy craft. Now the hunter becomes the hunted as the ship launches a salvo of missiles towards the Seahawk. The helicopter wheels to the right and heads down to the waves where the missiles lose its profile amongst the clutter of radar returns from the ocean's surface. The business of destroying the enemy now lies with the firepower of the task force and a concentrated missile attack completes the mission. The Seahawk returns to the area to assess the battle damage before turning back towards the Sydney and a landing on its pitching decks.

This was a simulation. However, the realism of the simulator and the proficiency of the crew very quickly drew me into the scenario as if it were real. And what I saw first hand was how a single helicopter can greatly increase the reach of a naval task force and provide a crucial source of eyes, ears and protection. To attain this level of crew proficiency is a challenging exercise and one that is constantly underway at their base at HMAS Albatross.

The Seahawk's crew of pilot, TACCO and Senso is an expert demonstration in crew co-ordination. Each member has a very specific role, however, in order to execute that duty efficiently they must also possess a keen understanding of the other roles. They must know when to speak and when to pause amidst an incredibly busy environment. Additionally, in the simulator I witnessed a high level of self-discipline by all the crew being exercised to maintain their defined roles and constantly revise their situational awareness as both individuals and as a team.

Central to the crew is the Aviation Warfare Officer (AvWO). Operating on board the Seahawk, the AvWO fills the role of TACCO and is the mission commander, responsible for the tactical employment of weapon and sensor systems, tactical communications, navigation and cockpit duties. Interestingly, as the Seahawk is flown single-pilot, the AvWo is also trained to back the pilot up to ensure the safety of the crew and the aircraft.

Petty Officer "Mac" McCallum followed the usual career path and was recruited from within the naval ranks to become a Senso. Now he has served actively abroad in a role that calls for him to gather and interpret information from the myriad sources carried by the Seahawk. Armed with that information, it must be translated and relayed to the crew in a concise and timely manner so that the TACCO can draw up and maintain a plan in a very dynamic setting.

For surface vessels, the SENSO relies heavily on radar and FLIR, while submarines call for the focus to fall upon acoustics.

Incredibly, the signals Mac receives can be cross-matched with known acoustic profiles to positively identify a craft by sound. That being said, the information is relayed with an appropriate classification as to the level of confidence in the identification.

Responding to this data and the plan drafted by the TACCO is the pilot, whose job it is to steer the Seahawk above the waves and deliver it safely back onto the deck of the ship. Like his counterparts, his language is very measured and always in the context of the full crew. He appreciates the intense workload that can fall upon his crewmates and realises that it is critical that he maintains an awareness of the big picture as he flies the helicopter. While the rest of the crew may be "head down" with their various duties, there is a need for the pilot to retain an overall situational awareness.

Maintaining a level of vigilance and look-out for unknown "contacts" and a constant appreciation of the Seahawk's fuel status are important tasks aside from flying the complex machine. Furthermore, the pilot must resist the temptation to get drawn deeply into the tactical situation that is developing as this may compromise the prime role of flying the helicopter. Once again, the theme resonates that these are highly trained individuals operating within a complex team situation.

The walls of the briefing room are adorned with maps of far-flung places and silhouettes of surface vessels. The rows of seats are filled with crews dressed in their green flight suits and dark brown leather jackets. In the front sits the Commanding Officer and his Executive Officer, or XO. A daily briefing of the meteorological situation, planned operations, current NOTAMS and other relevant information is followed by another detailed briefing of our individual sortie.

The pilot, Lieutenant Leigh George, briefs every aspect possible of our Seahawk flight, designated "Tiger 80". It is to be a complex flight, departing in company with a Bell 429 for an air-to-air photo session before heading further out to sea to disperse some flares and then firing the door-mounted 12.5mm machine gun. Finally, we will return to HMAS Albatross and my day will come to an end. Throughout the briefing, notes are jotted down by the crews and questions asked of Lieutenant George until, seemingly, no stone is left unturned.

As the crew make their way to the tarmac, I make a diversion to be fitted and equipped with a helmet and life vest. With the machine gun fitted to the Seahawk's open door, Lieutenant Starling kindly loans me his leather jacket, emblazoned with his ringed epaulettes and the Tiger crest of 816 Squadron. Helmet in hand, I can't help but feeling that perhaps I missed my true calling. On the tarmac, the Seahawk is being busily prepared with the TACCO, Lieutenant Geoff Winter inspecting the rotor head and the SENSO, Chief Petty Officer Ben Sime, attending to the machine gun. Sime is a man of few words but possesses an understated air of absolute competence. I am not surprised when I'm informed that he was awarded the Medal of Gallantry for his actions following a terrorist attack in 2004 while deployed to the Persian Gulf.

Lieutenant Winter shows me around the Seahawk, highlighting the various features from the FLIR to flares and the huge fuel tanks that afford the Seahawk its extended range. Despite the age of the helicopter and the nature of its operating environment, I am impressed with its appearance. It is yet another testimony to the crews, both in the air and on the ground.

CPO Sime briefs me on my actions in the event of an emergency before seating me near the radar screen that is the SENSO's domain. Meanwhile he straps in behind the pilot and after a series of checks the Seahawk's turbines begin to whine and we are underway.

The Bell 429 awaits our departure as we enter the hover above the threshold of Runway 26 before accelerating and climbing away from Albatross. It is mid-afternoon as the Bell 429 forms up on our port side and photographs the Seahawk as the coastline slips beneath us. I listen to the chatter between the TACCO and the pilot on this training sortie and the language is still clipped and efficient, verifying active restricted areas and assessing the weather and fuel status.

When the other helicopter peels away, the three crew members run through their drills before firing the flares from the Seahawk's flanks. The flares serve as a counter-measure against potential missile attacks and are launched from the aft fuselage section on either side. Initially, a lone flare is fired, mainly for my benefit in order to prepare my camera. Shortly afterwards, a brilliant salvo of streaking orange lights spray from either side of the Seahawk, with each trailing a white tail of efflux. Spectacular!

From here we fly further off-shore and Sime readies his machine gun, its barrel jutting out into the airflow. A smoke canister is dropped onto the water below to serve as a target as George brings the helicopter back around towards the target area. With every action the crew cross-checks and verifies. The distance and bearing of the target is verified and the safe/armed status of the weapon is communicated.

With the smoke sighted, George brings the Seahawk to bear and Sime readies to fire. The cracking of gunfire punches through my helmet and the smell fills my nose. Sime directs short, sharp bursts towards the target as the shell casings spray from the machine gun. I look beyond the barrel to see the telltale splashes of water rising about the ribbon of smoke. The accuracy of the fire is incredible and it is repeated on two subsequent passes, each time the process of checklists and calls is maintained.

Without a word, Sime secures the machine gun, checks the floor of the helicopter for any stray shell casings and straps back into his seat. He gives me a "thumbs up" to check that all is right with me and I return the gesture as the coastline returns to view all too quickly and the flight draws to a close.

After landing, Sime closes the side door and we taxi through the "bird bath" – a series of freshwater jets that hose the damaging saltwater from the airframe. The Seahawk shuts down and the rotors slow to a standstill. The gun is removed and taken away, leaving myself and Ben Sime to walk back across the tarmac to return my helmet and vest, and myself reluctantly to reality.

From my arrival at HMAS Albatross at 7:30am to the Seahawk parking on the flight-line at 4:30pm, it has been a busy day. I have glimpsed into the world of the naval aviator and what it takes to train a crew to a stage where it can be sent to sea with a huge amount of responsibility and minimal supervision.

The sincere philosophy of teamwork is one that emanated strongly from everyone I encountered – from the Commander of the Fleet Air Arm, Commodore Di Pietro CSC, RAN through to his men and women who fly and maintain the helicopters. There was a sense of mission that was universal, a pride in what had been achieved and a sense of anticipation for the times ahead.

Even so, the role of the Royal Australian Navy's helicopters still causes quizzical looks and draws questions from the broader community. Perhaps it was best put by Commodore Di Pietro when he said, "Naval aviation is what we do and the Fleet Air Arm is who we are". Personally, after a day at HMAS Albatross, I was left in no doubt as to the vital role performed by these men and women, quite literally on a global scale. A vital role that serves Australia proudly and deserves to emerge from beneath the radar.

***

37

IN THE HOVER

The only light for the past few nights has been the stars above my camouflaged tent, piercing the canopy formed by the towering trees that surround me. The long periods of silence have been broken by the occasional turbine spooling down or winding up as another helicopter discreetly comes or goes. I am in the field with an army squadron on exercise, far away from the comforts of the barracks.

Now, as dawn begins to break, there is movement beyond the canvas flap as the soldiers shuffle through the scrub and wheel their helicopters from their hiding places amongst the trees. The day is beginning and I drag myself upright and sit at the end of my stretcher. A splash of water and then the razor is reluctantly dragged across my stubbled face, with each sting making me a little more alert.

We meet in the shadow of the command post and share a joke and a cup of tea as we plunder our ration packs for breakfast. As the lone fixed-wing pilot, in this coterie of rotary-wing flyers, good-humoured sparring is the order of the day. However, the true test is only a short time away as I'll have my chance at the controls of a chopper and an opportunity to see if helicopters really do fly, or whether they simply beat the air into submission.

From breakfast to briefing, I follow the commanding officer who will fly the sortie today. The major, Tim, is highly experienced as both a pilot and a flight instructor. We pore over the charts to verify the boundaries of restricted airspace and the radio frequencies in use. The flight will be at a relatively low level for me, but at the heady heights of 200 feet or above for an army pilot. It will take us over the ridges and along the coastlines, and even make a call in at some jagged peaks.

Our Bell Kiowa has the call-sign of "Redback-One-Four" and sits on the northern edge of a small clearing that is serving as the squadron's forward operating base. The ground crew are flushing salt water out of the single-turbine engine atop the helicopter's cabin as Tim places his helmet and kit on the pilot's seat and readies the aircraft for flight. I tag along behind and listen to a detailed explanation of what makes the Kiowa tick. Many of the words are familiar to an aeroplane pilot, sharing the language of flight, but it is a slightly different dialect. Rotors, collective, torque, and tilting heads. By the time I strap into my seat, my head is spinning more quickly than the two blades that are now beginning to turn overhead, accelerating with every swipe of the air.

A good deal of Tim's face is concealed by the Gentex helmet and its dark tinted visor that reflects the world outside the cockpit quite clearly. A series of radio transmissions, a few words to me, a "thumbs up" and we're on our way. There is no need to taxi to a holding point, Tim merely increases power and raises a lever – the collective – and the flight begins. The blades of grass fall away from the Perspex beneath my feet and we are magically airborne without any run-up and forward leap into the sky. It's only a few feet of altitude, but we are in the air, magically motionless in space.

Here we sit momentarily as Tim feels left and right, up and down for the correct replies from the helicopter beneath his hands. Another scan of the instruments and, satisfied all is in order, he coaxes the Kiowa slowly forward and then a little faster and a little higher and a little faster, still. The tall trees at the far edge of the field loom large as we speed towards them, but then graciously defy gravity until we leave their olive leaves and twisted grey branches well beneath us.

With the helicopter's doors removed and the Perspex bubble in front of me only interrupted by a small central instrument panel, the outlook is phenomenal. The sense of free flight is amazing and, if not for the subtle thumping of the rotors above me, I almost believe I was suspended in mid-air and being gently pushed forward by the breeze. All the while, the outback scrub and trees sit a mere 200 feet below and I am hypnotised by the unimpeded view of their beauty.

Then a clearing appears beneath the nose of the Kiowa, with tall towers and a tethered blimp floating a few hundred feet in the air. On the ground lie a number of large, thin grey forms which Tim points out as UAVs, or "drones". He also points to the left, indicating that another UAV airfield lies a short distance away and that one of their breed has just become airborne. As we skirt the edge of the UAV's airspace, a small dot becomes steadily larger until I can distinctly make out the form of a UAV. I ponder the sight of being air-to-air with a pilotless craft; will this machine ultimately replace my breed?

The trees soon give way to mangroves and those in turn to the water's edge. With the coastline ahead, Tim hands control of the helicopter over to me for the first time and my eyes begin shifting between the beauty outside and the dials inside the cockpit. Altitude, airspeed, and vertical speed are all quite familiar, but now I have to include torque into my scan. I maintain 60 per cent torque, or power, through the collective lever in my left hand, while I fly the aircraft with the control-column, or "cyclic", in my right.

In forward flight, the helicopter is not that dissimilar to flying a conventional aeroplane, although it is a little more sensitive. Without a nose section ahead of me, I use a small nut on the cockpit's centre stanchion to hold a constant attitude relative to the horizon. Slowly my cycle of scanning and flying becomes more natural and I begin to enjoy cruising above the shallows. I sweep into a gentle turn to the left and then to the right, for no other reason than the fun of it.

A few pelicans pass down the left-hand side and then a huge turtle paddles beneath me. My eyes are now firmly outside as we fly towards the point of land ahead and I am free to take in the magic of my surroundings and the new world of helicopter flight. Everywhere that I look is untouched wilderness and wildlife, and the scent of that maritime world wafts in through the cockpit's open doorframe to the ever-present accompaniment of the rotors' *thump-thump-thump*.

Tim transmits to a naval vessel positioned off the coast for a clearance to continue our eastward course and into the restricted airspace. Without hesitation a voice booms back through my headsets informing us that we are cleared to operate along the coastline within certain defined boundaries which Tim re-confirms on the chart strapped to his thigh. He points ahead and I point the Kiowa.

We round the small headland and the scenery grows even more spectacular. Small islets with pristine pine trees sit just off the coast with small white waves breaking on their shore. I cruise along the white sands of the coast with the beach seeming to run beneath my feet; azure blue waters on my left and emerald green trees to my right. Every now and then a small secluded cove passes by, or a jagged rock inlet with crashing waves. The scene brings to mind pirates of old, hiding their masted galleons and dragging their treasure chests ashore. The setting is only interrupted by the occasional ripple of turbulent air bubbling over one of the rocky outcrops and burbling through my rotors overhead.

We climb away from the waves and the world around us becomes a far broader scene. Beyond the trees lie jagged volcanic pinnacles and the white sands now extend well beyond my view. It is picture-postcard perfect and Tim takes over to allow me to photograph the scene. He then offers to demonstrate the capabilities of this robust little helicopter and I accept the invitation with a broad smile.

He describes steep tactical climbs and descents to avoid small-arms fire that may be directed at the Kiowa from the ground as he slows the helicopter's forward flight. Not knowing what to expect, I grasp the doorframe in anticipation and to resist any temptation to grab the controls. Tim then smoothly noses the Kiowa over and the world below fills the Perspex ahead as we spear down towards the earth at 2,000 feet per minute. And then, as smoothly as we entered the descent, the nose is raised and we climb away from the imaginary threats at sea level and back into the heavens at 1,500 feet per minute. A sense of exhilaration overwhelms me, enhanced by an intimacy with the air afforded by the absent doors and the unlimited visibility of the helicopter's bubble-like cockpit.

After the rollercoaster, Tim cruises towards a rocky peak. Always aware of the wind's strength and direction he positions the Kiowa for an approach towards the jagged mountaintop. Slowly, we edge closer as the helicopter's flight transforms its bias from forward to vertical flight. I shift in my seat as an indicated airspeed of 10 knots would have a fixed-wing aircraft plummeting from the sky, but for the helicopter such a speed is normal. Inch by inch we draw closer to the peak, so close that I can see patches of lichen on the rocks and individual leaves fluttering on the limbs of the trees.

The helicopter responds to each minute movement of Tim's hands and feet as he re-enacts a manoeuvre that can deliver vital supplies or evacuate a critically ill patient from inhospitable terrain. I marvel at the skill of the pilot and the versatility of the machine as our landing skid sits motionless within feet of the ground below. It is sacrilege, but I am becoming converted to the ways of the rotary wing.

With low cloud rolling in and the wind speed increasing, we leave the world of peaks and pines behind, descending towards the coast once more. Safely away from the hills, I resume control of the Kiowa and reluctantly begin our transit back to the clearing that is the squadron's home. We retrace our steps over water and wildlife, across the coast and above the treetops. I am growing increasingly sensitive to the feel of the helicopter as I steer the machine along the route pointed out by Tim. I spot the tethered blimp of the UAV base and, after one more radio transmission, Tim takes over control and readies the helicopter to land back at base.

The clearing of the forward operating base comes into view, although we haven't begun to descend. Closer and closer we approach until the field is almost beneath our nose before Tim allows the helicopter to slow down. I recognise this manoeuvre and in an instant we are descending at 2,000 feet per minute on a tactical descent, parallel to the landing area. The helicopter then hauls around to the right in a steep turn, washing off energy and airspeed before levelling off; airfield ahead and we're "right on the numbers". Again I am impressed and the Kiowa now sits stationary in the "hover", 100 feet above the ground.

As I am to learn, in the hover the helicopter's controls change function. The control inputs no longer mimic those of a fixed-wing aircraft and a whole new set of skills is required to suspend the helicopter in space without drifting left or right, fore or aft, up or down. When Tim hands back over to me to hover the Kiowa, my thousands of hours in aeroplanes count for nought.

I am all at sea as I endeavour to master a skill more akin to balancing on a beach ball than flying. My instincts let me down and move me forward when I want to go down or slew me left when I want to turn. The trees surrounding the landing field look awfully close as I happily fumble my way around the three axes of movement without much success. My comfort zone shattered, Tim has a chuckle at the familiar struggle of the rookie and resumes control to fly the Kiowa smoothly down to the waiting fuel truck, and the flight comes to an end.

Hours later I am still catching my breath. I am impressed by the wide-ranging ability of the helicopter in the right hands, and a challenge has stirred within by its random manoeuvres when it attempted to hover in my hands. I share a ration pack and a joke with the Army pilots who gathered earlier to witness my inept hovering skills and now took the mandatory jabs at my ego. It is a long-held tradition of qualified helicopter pilots in the presence of their fixed-wing brethren and I take my medicine in good humour.

It is dark once more as I feel my way into my tent and lie down for the night. A whirring turbine starts once again and the telltale sound of the rotors turning begin shortly afterwards. Another Kiowa is about to take to the skies, but this time I am left on the ground to ponder. I consider the intimacy with which I have viewed the earth today and the way in which the helicopter allowed me to truly slow down and see the world, while my aeroplane might only offer a fleeting glance at speed. I recall the true freedom in space and the mastery of flight demonstrated by the major who flew beside me.

I settle back on my stretcher and my breathing slows. Perhaps flight has once again thrown down the gauntlet to a mere mortal like me. Perhaps there is now a new way for me to look at this beautiful world that surrounds us. Sleep now begins to take control. Perhaps there is a new life for me beyond today. A new life in the hover.

***

38

Pearl Harbor

I'm not flying. I'm a passenger.

The wheels are down and if I crane my neck I can see that the leading edge devices are fully extended along the wing outside. The landing into Honolulu is fast approaching, slowed only by the 30 knots of breeze on the nose. My eyes are firmly fixed outside.

There is an inlet, a small water mass, its neck widening as it moves inland from the coast. In the distance the profiles of naval vessels can be seen with their super-structures towering above the lowlands surrounding the harbour. I can see right up the valley extending to the north. It is picturesque, caught between two dramatically rising ridge lines.

Everywhere I look I see nature's beauty. In the volcanic peaks, or the moss-green fields that climb up their steep walls. The white beaches, jutting headlands, or the harbour that is home to these great ships. And yet, as scenic as it is, this harbour has a still higher significance. It is Pearl Harbor.

The site of the "day of infamy", it was in this harbour in December of 1941 that the historic Japanese attack took place. Launched from distant aircraft carriers, the airborne armada set out to catch the American fleet in port and disable America's capability to combat the Empire's advance through Asia. The American aircraft carriers were at sea, but in a devastating blow, the battleship fleet was massacred on their moorings.

The Japanese attacked in two waves that quiet Sunday morning. American air superiority was crippled, caught on the ground in neat little rows. By the end, more than 2,000 Americans were dead with over 1,000 of these lost in the sinking of a single ship, the USS Arizona.

Now as I cast my eye over this innocent-looking landscape, I see much more than the scenery. Books, movies and documentaries have burned this place into the world's consciousness and mine is no exception. I imagine the plumes of smoke billowing up from the stricken vessels and the Japanese torpedo-bombers skimming low above the water towards their goal. Fighters fill the sky and dive-bombers howl down towards the decks of those ships deeper inside the harbour, obscured from the torpedoes' paths. There is chaos, suffering, heroism and destruction.

The majority of those who would fight and die were mere boys, well less than half my age. The war had arrived with lethal ferocity and no apparent warning on a quiet morning when flags were being raised and church services organised. It was a war that would last for years and reach right around the world for the Americans. It would span the islands of the Pacific and across North Africa and Europe where the allies had been suffering since 1939. It was now truly a world war.

Today the scene is almost idyllic. Gardens and memorials line the harbour's foreshore to honour the memory of those lost on that fateful morning. The remains of the USS Arizona and its crewmen still lie just beneath the surface with a dribble of oil still occasionally coming to the surface. Some say these are the tears of the lost sailors below. This is sacred ground and a pervasive air of reverence envelopes the location.

Nearby, another great battleship sits at anchor, the USS Missouri. Under construction in New York at the time the Arizona was lost, the Missouri saw action in World War Two, Korea and as recently as the Persian Gulf, before coming home to rest in Pearl Harbor. Upon its flanks a Kamikaze pilot met his end and on her decks the Japanese signed the surrender document in 1945. It now sits at Pearl Harbor as a towering reminder of all that took place before. Along with the Arizona, it provides a pair of "bookends" to the Pacific war. The Arizona lost on that first fateful day for the United States, while the Missouri bore witness to the war's end in Tokyo Bay.

Pearl Harbor now slides by and the grass and sand is replaced by the black asphalt of an airport apron. Row after row of grey American aircraft slide by outside and hangars proudly announce their address. Military blends into civil and, finally, sky into earth. The rigid windsock flashes past and the wheels settle upon the runway. We have arrived.

For me this is a holiday. A short break. I will wander the shores and watch the sun set on Waikiki Beach, rest and recharge. Yet, only a few miles away is the scene of one of modern history's most significant moments. The smoke plumes have now gone, but the sense of loss is as strong as ever for both this island and the nation of which it is a part. I will pay my respects and contemplate those who were lost amongst these gentle waves and swaying palms. And maybe I'll even glimpse those tears floating to the surface. Regardless, for me Pearl Harbor is no longer present in the pages of history books alone. It is now something real in my heart.

Lest We Forget.

***

39

A Ghost in the Machine?

Thirty years ago, the careers guidance counsellor at my school suggested that I investigate a future in the leisure industries. His skewed logic was that the growth of computers would overrun the workforce, availing people of a mountain of free time in which they would need to be entertained. So how's that working out for everyone?

He also warned me off a career in aviation as by the year 2000 since pilots would be increasingly redundant as automation replaced the man in the cockpit. Fortunately, I ignored all of his recommendations and pursued my chosen vocation in the air. Even so, his apocalyptic vision for pilots is coming a lot closer than his prediction regarding computers. Automation has indeed encroached heavily into the pilot's domain and the growth of technology such as Unmanned Aerial Vehicles (UAV) is no longer futuristic.

Early steps in the pilot's fall from grace could be seen in the disappearance of their former comrades; the navigators and flight engineers. With the advent of autonomous navigation systems and automated power management, two crucial members of the flight deck have disappeared into obscurity. Only a small fleet of older-generation aircraft and some specialised operations still call for a "nav" or "FEO". And so the role of the pilot has diminished, offering up numerous manual tasks to onboard computers.

That role has evolved into a more managerial position, where crews, systems and aircraft are overseen rather than "handled". The "stick and rudder" skills became less crucial as autopilots were able to perform the task, freeing up the pilot's brain-space to oversee the greater operation and maintain heightened situational awareness. The captains of Ernest Gann's books letting down on the NDB to the sound of rain thrashing against the fogging windscreen are rapidly becoming something of folklore. Today it is autopilot, auto-coupled and auto-landed, and with the technology rapidly flowing downhill into small single-pilot operations, the evolution is being witnessed across the full spectrum of aircraft.

Perhaps the most notable impact upon the brotherhood of pilots can be seen in UAVs. Rather than having pilots perched at the sharp end of the aircraft, they are seated at a ground-based console flying the aircraft remotely. Crews can be based in a mobile control van, or seated in a room on the other side of the planet. In any case, they are far removed from their UAV when it is 'on station' and potentially in harm's way. When the first unmanned Global Hawk flew non-stop from the United States to Australia in 2001, it highlighted that these vehicles had definitely come of age. With a range in excess of 12,000nm, a ceiling of 65,000 feet and an ability to remain aloft for periods in excess of 30 hours, the Global Hawk demonstrated immense potential to survey and gather data or intelligence.

Yet surveillance has proven to be only one of many roles suited to the UAVs. No longer merely "drones", these vehicles are able to patrol borders, carry remote sensing equipment relaying information about the atmosphere or fly into the heart of tornadoes where no sane pilot would venture. They possess a potential to transport goods or provide assistance to search-and-rescue teams with onboard thermal sensors or cameras. These UAVs may be fixed wing in form, or rotary wing.

Yet it is in theatres of war that the Unmanned Combat Aerial Vehicles (UCAV) are attracting the most headlines. Heavily armed

UCAVs have had an impact on operations in global hot-spots such as Afghanistan and are rewriting the way that warfare is conducted. Carrying sensors and cameras, the UCAV has nasty teeth, paired with pinpoint precision targeting and without the need for exposing a pilot or his aircraft to the associated danger.

While UCAVs currently fly alongside piloted combat aircraft, is the day coming when all combat aircraft are unmanned? Immune to physiological limitations, g-forces won't render this aircraft unconscious in a tight turn, and there is not a human life in harm's way. Will the absence of a human life in the cockpit change the way in which our leaders decide to deploy the force at their fingertips?

So is this the future of all aviation; faceless and guided by a remote hand? It is apparent that we are already moving steadily in that direction. The common catchcry in civil aviation is that passengers won't board a flight without a human crew "up the front", yet passengers happily commute around Paris on trains that are void of drivers. Culture rather than technology is shaping up as the key architect of this brave new world.

In aviation, science fiction has a long history of rapidly evolving into science fact. Whether we see human faith in automation mature to the extent that oceans are crossed without pilots on the flight deck will only be revealed in time. However, we are already seeing unmanned vehicles performing admirably in a diverse range of roles that could once only have been imagined. How long this will take is yet to be seen, but already there is little doubt that we are witnessing the growth of the ghost in the machine.

***

40

THE RIGHT MIX

Tom Wolfe's book made "the right stuff" famous and then the film rocketed the phrase and the concept to an entirely new level. It was meant to describe that intangible quality that separates elite aviators from those of us that sit back in the pack. Strangely enough, as every year passes I find the "right stuff" increasingly difficult to discover beyond the realm of the test and fast jet pilots. Even so, a good many aviators still bounce the term around, seemingly out of context.

Personally, I thoroughly enjoyed the film. Despite the Hollywood slant on the events surrounding the breaking of the sound barrier and the Mercury astronauts, it was exciting entertainment and great viewing. It brought the story home to a new generation that were virtually ignorant of the events that transpired as man pushed the limits of flight.

I've shared many a conversation with fighter pilots of that same era and the vast majority ranked luck as the prime requirement for survival. In combat and in flying the first generation of jet fighters, they had a litany of tales of how they almost broke their necks through ignorance and stupidity. They watched good friends make the same mistakes, only to leave a crater in some remote field.

Furthermore, they would recount fellow pilots who had the qualities that were perceived as having the right stuff. They were "natural" pilots with superior stick-and-rudder skills and unflappable confidence. They earned top marks and won the trophies and accolades and were envied by their peers. Yet as these old, greying pilots continued to chat, they would recall how a good many of these wonderful pilots had died while flying.

They had been killed pushing on in bad weather, executing a low-level manoeuvre that just didn't work or taking the aircraft a little further than the designers had seen as prudent. The pilots I spoke to offered over-confidence and complacency as factors in the demise of these talented flyers, but as always, bad luck played its hand too.

These old pilots were never critical of their talented comrades who had died doing what they loved. Sometimes, pausing as if for the first time, they could see a link between ability and mortality. Perhaps they would shrug their shoulders or raise an eyebrow, but little more. After all, it was a dangerous vocation back then.

The majority of these ageing aviators held themselves in far less regard. "I was very average" and "I got through by the skin of my teeth" were common expressions from this generation of pilots who had literally been there and done that. They saw themselves as fortunate survivors rather than "aces", and to me this seemed strange.

Perhaps the right stuff lay more in recognising the limits than pushing them. These gentlemen had flown hundreds of combat sorties between them and been amongst the first to fly jets. They had done everything that could be asked of them and survived, and yet all they saw in the mirror was an average pilot with luck on his side.

When I consider the modern generation of pilots that I have flown with, I find common ground with these pilots of the past. The demographics of air crews are fairly standard, and recruiting processes look to maintain that. A few individuals step out of the box, but generally speaking there is similarity amongst the breed that is pulled more closely together by standard operating procedures in a disciplined workplace. There are gifted pilots, but a greater number are average and live from one simulator check to the next. They are always their own toughest critic and lament how they could have flown so much better. In their eyes they just get by, it's the other guy who has the right stuff.

To be a pilot you don't need to be special, just the right sort of person for the job. A degree of flying ability is required, but so too is a level of proficiency in interfacing with technology and interacting with other people. Rather than possessing one single quality, it is about a balance of a few. It's about keeping them in proportion and shifting them in priority as the situation dictates at the time.

Being strong in one area and weak in another is far from an ideal situation. The best manipulative pilot needs to be able to master the automation and the pilot who plays the technology like a keyboard must also know when it is time to hand-fly the aeroplane. And as good as they are in either situation, they must be able to work with those around them.

Fellow pilots, cabin crew, engineers and ground staff are all valued components in the complex aviation cycle. Drawing upon these valuable resources and communicating effectively across the board can be as challenging as any skill a pilot may need and as critical as any need they may encounter.

Reflecting upon the wealth of knowledge of experienced aviators I have known as well as my own time aloft, I am still no closer to truly understanding the right stuff. I've always perceived it as an intangible quality, so perhaps I am destined to never get any closer to the heart of the matter. Regardless, I don't believe that it is a single quality. I think it is a blend of traits that are brought to the fore or tucked away as needed.

The right stuff? I honestly don't know. There are pilots whose job it is to push aircraft to the limits, but they are the elite test and fighter pilots who are trained to do just that. For most of us mere mortals, we do not and should not tear at the edge of the envelope. Perhaps, for the majority, the necessary qualities are not so much the right stuff as the right mix.

***

A Bell 'Kiowa' as seen through Night Vision Goggles. (NVG).

Something Different. The 'Cozy' peels away. (Image: 'Australian Aviation')

41

SOMETHING DIFFERENT

It was time for something completely different. I am always keen to get up close with any type of aeroplane I can, but I had never had the opportunity to fly a canard. I hadn't flown the combination of the pusher propeller, horizontal stabiliser in front and all the other weird and wonderful traits that accompany the type. The Cozy Mark IV was my opportunity.

The first time I encountered the Cozy was in the climate-controlled shed of its owner/builder Chris Byrne. From the outset I could sense that this was an aircraft with a difference. It was not a "kit plane" and its construction did not involve the assembly of prefabricated components; rather it was moulded from the ground up. From nothing more than a set of plans, rolls of woven fibreglass had been carefully layered with epoxy. While PVC foam sheets formed the bulkheads and fuselage sides, urethane foam was used to form highly curved, hand-carved shapes such as the nose and wing tips, and ultimately created the unique shape that defines the aircraft. Readying this creation to take to the skies involved around 3,500 man-hours, wedged in between work and family commitments. I was in awe of the building effort as much as the aeroplane's smooth lines.

When it came time to fly, the day was unfriendly and overcast. Fundamentally, the aeroplane is a 4-place canard with a single "pusher" engine at the rear and topped with a front-hinged bubble canopy. The small, lifting canard at the front is home to the elevators, and the mainplane's large winglets integrate the aeroplane's rudders. It sounds topsy-turvy by conventional standards, and with baggage pods resembling "drop tanks" beneath each wing, this aircraft's futuristic form would seemingly be well at home as one of Batman's modes of transport. Still, I couldn't wait to fly it.

Despite its striking form, the pre-flight inspection was quite conventional other than weight and balance calculations that can call for ballast in the nose. However, there were no flaps but there was a belly-mounted speedbrake. The nose gear can be fully, or partially, lowered or raised on the ground and the aircraft is easily manoeuvred around the hangar by a heavily reinforced, nose-mounted pitot tube. It goes against every instinct to place weight on the pitot, but when this is overcome there is very little pushing or panting in handling the Cozy.

I hopped up, backside-first, onto the leading edge and then swung my legs down into the cockpit. It wasn't too challenging, however it might get a bit tougher after another 20 football seasons. The aircraft is definitely Cozy by both name and nature, but harnessed in you could also describe it as comfortable.

We lowered the large canopy and very soon the Lycoming engine was brought to life. Compliments of the aft-mounted engine and three-bladed pusher propeller, the cockpit was remarkably quiet. As we taxied out, its futuristic form stirred people from their hangars and even had cars pulling over on the nearby roadside.

Yet, for all of the small pre-flight idiosyncrasies of ballast requirements, folding nosewheels and pitot probe handling systems, once you open the throttle this machine is all aeroplane. We accelerated briskly along the sealed surface. Approaching 70 knots you feel the canard start to fly and the aircraft burst into life. Chris warned me that this needed to be tempered by gentle forces in the rotation or the aircraft rears its head as it leaps into the air. And did it leap!

The Cozy was absolutely beautiful to fly in the turn, rolling around the sky effortlessly. With the bubble canopy surrounding us and the swept wing positioned well behind, the visibility was absolutely breathtaking. It was like the spectacular view afforded by any bubble canopy, but this aircraft didn't even have a significant nose or spinning propeller out in front.

We whistled up through the clouds at 155 knots with the sporty control stick sitting in my left hand. The speedbrake control is on the side-stick and deploying the speedbrake is akin to lowering a small barn door from beneath the aeroplane and the speed washes off accordingly. You can also slow down by depressing both rudder pedals and deflecting both rudders outboard, resulting in no roll or yaw, but another source of drag. This mechanism is available at any speed and is very effective in slowing down or increasing the rate of descent. The designers obviously recognised that this may be an aircraft that needs a hand to slow down.

Cozy advertise that the aircraft is very "stall resistant" and I would have to agree. Without flaps I throttled back and slowed towards the 70-knot mark. There was some buffeting before the nose gently pitched down, then rose, and then gently pitched down again. With the control column continually held fully back, this cycle of undulations is about as violent as one of those oscillating rides for kids that they have in shopping centres. With the power reintroduced and the stick held fully back, the aircraft continued to gently porpoise but arrested the descent and ultimately started to gain altitude. Stall resistant indeed! This rather different flight profile is the result of the canard stalling and then unstalling; the wings do not actually reach the stall.

Joining the circuit at our destination, the Cozy again grabbed centre-stage as the apron filled with bodies emerging from the hangars. Through a combination of extended landing gear and reduced power, I managed to slow down to 95 knots before turning back towards the field and commencing descent. Reducing to 90 knots on final and targeting 85 knots on touchdown, even these few knots have to be bled off early if speedbrake is not used. Chris warns me that the aircraft wants to float, so I make sure that I'm on speed over the fence and my aim point is right on the money; then I flinch. My thoughts of flaring translate into muscle movement and I pull back slightly on the stick. Yep, this aeroplane wants to float. Obeying my philosophy of "if in doubt, bug out", I advanced the throttle, set the attitude and climbed away before retracting the gear and returning for a second attempt. With no flaps on the wings, a go-around in the Cozy is as simple as they come.

The ground fell away rapidly and, in a blink, I was back in the circuit and making calls and completing checks. I mentally reviewed the previous attempt and briefed myself that very little flare is needed to land this aeroplane. I reminded myself of this point again on final approach and checked that the speed was on the numbers. This time the runway slipped by beneath me and the landing worked out nicely, but I admit to concentrating very intently to make it happen.

After flying a number of takeoffs and landings, we waved to the people on the apron and set course for home. Above us the grey overcast sat steadily so we decided to fly home visually in the clear air beneath the cloud base. The motorway plotted our course and I was free to fly this sweet machine and navigate by following the cars. It was effortless in every sense of the word and all the while I looked about my 360-degree view in wonder.

Ahead of me, the moving map beckoned and the autopilot longed to be engaged, but there was a sheer joy of flying to be had. With every sweeping turn, the view along the swept leading edge to the winglet-rudders was a view that I had never seen before. It was very different to every other Piper, Cessna and Beechcraft, but it was not alien; I felt right at home. With its speed and comfortable noise levels, I longed to really stretch the Cozy's legs and fly the aeroplane cross-country. It is built to tour and let the pilot drink in the scenery unobscured by windshield pylons or propeller blades.

All too soon we were home to the familiar hills and paddocks. The airfield's brown edges contrasted with the green fields and aided the eye to sight the runway at a distance. We sped into the circuit and wheeled about the pattern without another aircraft to be seen or heard. Again I reminded myself of the numbers and the aircraft's propensity to keep flying as the landing gear is lowered and final preparations are made.

The runway lies ahead, as cattle and the occasional rooftop passes by in my peripheral vision. The old barbed wire fence with the painted white tyres marks the airfield's perimeter and soon the threshold was passing beneath my wheels. Throttle closed, no flinching and we have returned to earth in a respectable fashion with lots of runway to spare.

Outside the hangar, the canopy rises slowly and it seems as though we have been flying in a spaceship that would be found in the cartoon series, "The Jetsons". However, this is a real aeroplane; less conventional than most, but truly enjoyable to fly. I take in the uncluttered perspective around me one more time before I slide off the wing's leading edge and call it a day. Once again, people emerge from their hangars and cars parked by the airfield fence, keen to see the Cozy. Keen to see something that is completely different.

***

42

WELCOME HOME

I have said many times that aviation can be as much about the people as it is about the aeroplanes. Remarkable people who fly through the night to aid others, or wise old souls who pass their wisdom onto a new generation. Then there are the adventurers who criss-cross the globe in light aircraft and from their numbers come a very special few. Ryan Campbell is one of those individuals...

The aerobatic team has departed, the crowd has dissipated and the Cirrus SR22 now sits quietly in the hangar receiving some well-earned attention. Ryan is home from his solo flight around the world and has had a few days to allow reality to sink in. Even so, one senses that he won't be resting for long and there are still other horizons that he seeks to conquer. It all seems very surreal to him. As he sits in his home on the Australian east coast, after returning from what would be an epic adventure in anyone's language. At 19 years of age he has become the youngest person to fly solo around the world.

Given a hero's welcome and even a feature on TV's *60 Minutes*, Ryan has hardly had time to catch his breath, let alone reflect on his flight to any great extent in the days since his return. It has been a whirlwind, but more than that it has been the fruition of years of planning. Behind the scenes there was a huge learning curve as Ryan sought to put the logistics in place to support such an ambitious undertaking.

He had to learn about tax laws and contend with an unexpected aircraft change only weeks before departure. Dealing with the media, seeking permits, locating suppliers and fundraising for his nominated charity were just a few of the tasks that were far from the skies, but still vital to the flight's success. Ultimately, his triumphant return was really the culmination of both a global circumnavigation and the many less glamorous tasks that allowed it to take place.

Even along the way, unforeseen hurdles arose. The unsettled political environment and unfolding violence cast a shadow over the Egyptian leg of the flight. From the time he was in the United States, the situation was worsening and yet he took each day at a time, concentrating on the flight at hand with one eye on Egypt. When he was in Greece he finally, and reluctantly, decided to divert around the land of the pharaohs. Even this decision bore added pressure as the Egyptian Consulate attempted to change his mind.

Consequently, as I now begin to chat with Ryan about his flight, he shares a sincere sense of relief. A weight has been lifted from his shoulders as he was always aware that, for all of the great support he received, the ultimate fate of the flight rested with him. And while he took every step to mitigate problems that may arise, the spectre of a very public failure was always there. Only when he touched down back at Albion Park Airport was that burden lifted. But, in the end, it was all well worth it and he'd enjoyed many special moments along the way.

Fitting your life into the back of a light aircraft laden with ferry tanks is no small undertaking in itself. Ryan soon became expert at surviving with minimal luggage and rolling clothes into ever-tightening spaces. Spare parts were at a premium with the spark plugs, filters and oil being priorities, and the oil proving to be rather heavy.

He wore a life jacket at all times over water and a bulky immersion suit for his crossing of the North Atlantic. His constant companion on the seat beside him was "Bob" – an inflatable life raft. His flight spanned a temperature range from -9 degrees to 45 degrees Celsius, and saw him breathe oxygen through nasal prongs as the Cirrus spanned the Pacific Ocean at Flight Level 130. Both man and machine were exposed to a range of operating environments, but in the 170 hours aloft, there those special moments.

So special, in fact, that Ryan does not hesitate as he rattles off a handful that stand out from the others – for a range of differing reasons. Firstly, there were the lights of Santa Barbara emerging from the darkness and the sea fog loitering along the United States' coastline. In this case they were not just the warming glow of another city; they marked the completion of one of the journey's most challenging sectors.

Fifteen hours earlier he had lined up in the darkness at Hilo Airport in Hawaii with over 2,200 nautical miles of ocean ahead of him. The challenge was daunting as he advanced the throttle and set the Cirrus on its way into the night sky. The sun rose and set again faster than he had ever seen; all the while he calculated his speed and fuel consumption on this critical leg.

The winds were not quite as favourable as had been forecast. He took the aircraft from 9,000 feet to 11,000 feet and then to 13,000 feet looking for friendlier winds and better fuel consumption. All the while his point-of-no-return grew closer, at which time he'd have to decide to return to Hawaii or accept that he was committed to continue on to the US mainland. A little more ground speed and with tailwinds predicted to kick in a few hours ahead, the calculation was complete. Ryan would continue. After hours of tense calculations, miles of ocean and darkness, the lights of Santa Barbara were a sight he would never forget.

In contrast, the busy skies of the Airventure Air Show at Oshkosh were a far cry from sitting alone over the Pacific Ocean. A line of 20 aircraft, all funnelling into the Wisconsin Airport and being steered towards the dot on the runway that marked their landing point. Despite hours of watching videos and researching the arrival, the sea of parked aircraft and the sight of his own green dot in the windscreen was an exciting moment for the young pilot.

History overcame the excitement when he crossed the English Channel. Looking down on the White Cliffs of Dover and turning towards France, he could almost see the ancient Armadas as he passed through the very same airspace where Spitfires and Messerschmitts had once duelled. A place that had once only existed in his Australian schoolbooks was now sweeping beneath his own wings.

Closer to home, the sight of crystal waters rolling against the shoreline at Broome was the final special moment Ryan spoke of without pausing. Australia – his homeland. Even though there was still some way to travel, crossing the Australian coast meant that he was back on his home turf and the scenery, food, airspace and friendly faces were familiar and comforting. The journey was nearly over, he could almost taste it.

As Ryan set out from Broken Hill bound for Wollongong on that final day, the crown was already gathering to meet him. The RAAF Roulettes formation team were putting on a display as he worked his way across NSW and I even managed to have a word with him from my flight deck at 38,000 feet. At the time Ryan was hundreds of miles away being pushed along by a substantial tailwind.

Normally, tailwinds are a good thing and, during that long haul from Hawaii, I'm sure Ryan would have been wishing for them. However, when a finely timed and choreographed welcome home event has been planned, it can throw the schedule out somewhat. As a consequence, the young solo pilot was left with some time on his hands, so he dawdled a little to the west of Sydney with his final destination tantalisingly close.

There was still an air-to-air photographic sequence to complete, so he wheeled about the sky void of any pressure as he waited for the helicopter and its camera crew to arrive. All the while, excited family, friends and a growing crowd looked skywards for any hint of the Cirrus in the cloudless sky.

When the helicopter approached from the east it was yet another highlight for Ryan. After so many hours aloft and alone over recent weeks, the sight of another aircraft close by and there to greet him was exhilarating. The relative motion of the two aircraft as they passed by, set to the backdrop of the Australian countryside, reminded Ryan in the nicest of ways that the journey was drawing to a close. After a series of shots from a broad range of angles, he parted company with the helicopter. Once again his sights were set on Wollongong and he set heading for the "steel city".

His level of elation had risen somewhat when he flew in company with the camera ship, but his heart almost leapt from his chest as he crossed the escarpment and Wollongong lay ahead. If the footage ever surfaces, Ryan suggests watching his face as he turned base leg before landing as his excitement poured forth, before concentrating on a decent landing in front of a thousand waiting cameras.

His skill and the fickle hand of fate delivered the smoothest of touchdowns before he taxied his trusty Cirrus between a vee formed by the Royal Australian Air Force's parked scarlet Pilatus PC-9s. The propeller stopped and he climbed out on the wing to rousing cheers. He was reunited with his rightly proud parents and his team of supporters as reporters waited their turn for a word with the world traveller. For his part, Ryan was most touched by the sea of excited children that just wanted to touch the aeroplane that had been all the way around the world. In many ways, their excitement and dreams was what the flight and now the journey ahead is all about.

Towering cumulonimbus clouds and floating icebergs, lonely outposts and buzzing cities, Ryan has seen them all. Those images are fixed in his memory, but now his focus is firmly on the future. He wants to share his amazing journey and inspire youngsters across Australia. Ideally he would like to fly around the nation to visit schools, but insists that he'll drive if he has to. I've learned that determination is a strong character trait in Ryan.

Before he ever set out on his flight, Ryan saw himself as a yes-or-no person. Once his mind is set on a course of action he will commit to it 100 per cent and succeed or go down fighting. He also expressed how the flight put his commitment to the test. If he had decided to build an aeroplane in his Dad's shed, then he could have thrown the spanner down and watch TV whenever it got too tough. However, publically proclaiming that you're going to fly solo around the world leaves nowhere to hide.

Ryan has many projects underway and ideas racing through his mind. He is an inspiring young man to listen to and his genuine commitment to the task means that a boundless future lies ahead. In commercial aviation, corporate jets and warbirds have caught his eye, but I am sure there is even more in store down the road. For the moment, Ryan deserves to relax for awhile to reflect and enjoy the weight lifting from his shoulders. To catch up with friends and ponder his future. Being the youngest person to fly solo around the world is a dream that Ryan made sure came true. Personally, I can't wait to see what comes next.

Welcome home, Ryan.

***

43

A Fighter's World

The speck becomes a silhouette, then a roar and then it's gone. Just a whisper is left lingering as the ribbons of disturbed air dance above our heads.

The scene is repeated time after time as the FA-18 "Hornet" fighter jets return to base, each flying over our vantage point before rejoining the runway in a puff of burnt rubber. My young son stares towards the coast in anticipation of each arrival, torn between plugging his ears with his fingers and trying to yell above the noise of the screaming jets. He chooses the latter and cranes his head back to breaking point as another jet approaches with its wheels and flaps extended. For him, it's the best show in town.

Finally the last Hornet touches down and clears the runway, leaving the sky eerily silent after such a frenzy. In the distance, a sedate airliner begins to taxi away from the terminal, but it holds none of the same allure for my five-year-old. He scans the sky again, as if another fighter will magically appear, but none are forthcoming. In minutes the airfield has transformed from an action-filled terminus to just another airport, and the barbed wire on the fence-line seems hardly worth the effort. But this is not just another airport; it is the home to Australia's jet fighter force and, in a bygone era, the home to my son's grandfather. A man who once also looked skyward as old Air Force biplanes flew overhead, determined to emulate them one day.

In walking distance from where we are standing, a large hangar is conspicuous amongst the surrounding buildings. Its roof arcs in a large scarlet span and its doors are painted blue with an image of a Hornet seemingly bursting through and into the daylight. "Fighter World" is emblazoned in massive letters across those doors and there is no mistaking what must lie within these walls. This is the place where a fortunate few old jets retire when their days on the edge of the envelope are over. All four of my children rush towards the entrance and I am certain that the possibility of a gift shop is as tempting a lure as the impressive array of flying hardware. Either way, I am just as eager as they are as we enter the building, greeted by a sea of proud paint schemes and towering tailplanes.

Wedged in, wingtip to wingtip, the fighter jets are corralled in close quarters. It is a far cry from the wide open skies that they once tore apart at the speed of sound. Still, they have survived, and that's what matters. Unlike their squadron mates, they have not been melted down into scrap or met an ignominious end, forgotten and rotting on an airfield's perimeter. Here they are cared for and their stories recounted on boards designed to both educate the visitor and celebrate the veteran pilots. The walls are adorned with artwork, and squadron badges and mottos sit atop plaques and displays. History oozes from every corner and between the artefacts are personal anecdotes that paint the human face.

My children queue to climb into decommissioned cockpits, to push and pull every switch and lever that will move. They sink deeply into the massive ejection seat and stand no chance of seeing above the instrument panel and gunsight ahead of their small faces. Even so, they are content to fly blind and allow their imaginations to paint the image of clouds flicking past and the horizon tumbling wildly. They move from jet to jet, climbing steps and peering down into the confines of the resting fighters. When the canopies are closed, they cup their hands and peer up through the Perspex and at the maze of dials and gauges. The early, primitive jets had their heyday between the pinnacle of the propeller era and the dawn of the new technology. The cockpit is characterised by black-and-white panels and placards, and an absence of logical layout. The only true constants are the throttle and the control column.

These jets did evolve and at quite a pace. Their straight wings became swept back and the sound barrier was no longer a brick wall in the sky. Afterburners pushed them ever faster and the weaponry became increasingly clever. But still a special kind of pilot was needed to fill the lone seat. A pilot with the same blood as the knights of the skies in World War One and whose traditions have been passed down through the generations. And regardless of what Hollywood may wish to portray, there is no true stereotype of the fighter pilot. There may be common traits and skills, but the cliché portrayal of the "Top Gun" belies the true qualities that matter.

Among the wheels and wings, the canopies and the cannons, one aircraft is personally significant. Its markings speak its name, but not its story. This very jet is one that my father flew. The Gloster Meteor with its two wing-mounted jet engines, "bubble" canopy and nose cannons, sits beside its successor, the sleek Avon Sabre. My children clamber up the small stairs and pose for a photograph beside their "grandad's jet". The four of them smile proudly in the warmth of a physical connection to a man that they never knew. It is a significant moment for me as I frame the photograph in my camera, but it is evaporates when the walls begin to shake.

The roar of the Hornets has returned as they take off on another sortie, and my children take off upstairs and onto an outside viewing platform. At regular intervals and in pairs, the Hornets take to the sky before heaving into a turn and skirting just above the horizon. Soon they can no longer be seen. Two by two they scream skyward, their afterburners yelling defiantly at the unsuccessful efforts of gravity to contain them. They are thoroughbreds champing at the bit and running free until time and technology finally pushes them into the corner of a hangar for children and tourists to contemplate.

My children grapple with the railing in an attempt to gain a better view of the spectacle, although one of them is not here. I count heads one more time before I peer back into the relative darkness of the hangar. My eldest daughter is still standing beside the Meteor, gazing down into the cockpit. I quietly move down the stairs and stand some distance away, contemplating her thoughtful little face. It is as if she is looking through time, her chin resting on the cockpit's edge and contemplating her own special fighter pilot. In her mind is he sitting there? Strapped in, oxygen mask and helmet fitted, his hands on the throttle and "stick"? Despite the temptation of the noise and excitement outside, she never left her grandad's side. I'd like to think that wherever he is now, that he will never leave hers.

***

44

No Escape

My resolution was quite clear. I would take a break from flying and a short sabbatical from writing and leave the laptop computer and my "flight bag" at home to ensure that happened. An aviator's "cold turkey". A few days away to unwind and recharge after a hectic month of deadlines and destinations. Well, that was the plan.

The opportunity had arisen to fly with my wife to a distant island with swaying palms, soft music and bamboo torches burning on the beach at sunset. Okay, I had to catch a flight to get there, but I'd just be a passenger, so that doesn't count; no laptops, no licences. In fact, the trip would give me a chance to read those books that I'd been wanting to finish. I was content that this would be a break to remember and, as we pushed back from the terminal in darkness and the Boeing's engines turned over, I was well at ease.

Soon the runway lights were flashing past at increasing speed and then falling away altogether. They were soon replaced by the landing lights illuminating the cloud until we broke through to the clear night above. The landing lights extinguished, only the blinking strobes and twinkling stars interrupted the blackness of the night.

Somewhere over the Pacific I peeked out the window and distant flashes reminded me that the tropics were alive and well. Their rising air masses and moisture were bubbling even without the sun there to heat them and shards of lightning provide a stark warning. The sun rose with pace and the first red rays were soon replaced by the brightness of day, rousing my fellow travellers.

The rumbling of extending leading edges and thumping of the landing gear lowering were the first aural disturbances in nearly nine hours aloft. Outside my window a lower level of occasional cumulus was all that interrupted the view down to the rolling waves and the massive vessels stirring up their wake.

The sandy coastline swept beneath me and rich green volcanic peaks and craters were everywhere to be seen. A runway here and another there and a range of old warbirds sitting on a greying tarmac. It is a military museum I gather and soon its confines give way to living, breathing military aircraft. Row upon row of C-17 Globemasters and KC-35 "Tankers" fill the window while a row of F-22 "Raptors" is being readied for the day ahead. Even as they sit dormant on the ground their form is both impressive and intimidating.

Our wheels hit the runway and I hit the customs hall. Two hours later I am clear of the airport, waist deep in crystal clear water and finally free of flight. I immerse myself in the water as fish swim around me and the cleanest of sand slips between my toes. A line of airliners launch above me one after the other at an incredible rate. There are coloured tails of airlines that I have never seen and the forms of jets that have long ceased frequenting my homeland. It's a passing parade of interesting aircraft turning left and right and setting course for exotic destinations.

Lower down helicopters full of tourists skip along the beach before torque-turning back to whence they came. Brightly coloured with scarlet and orange stripes, they are distinctly different from the thumping of the camouflaged military choppers that thump past me. There seems to be an absence of single-engined piston aeroplanes but an abundance of turbo-prop Cessna Caravans. Perhaps those rugged hills and craters are best seen from behind a turbine I ponder.

Later, I trek in the heat to the base of one of the craters and through a tunnel to reach the deep bowl of vegetation within. Here the air is still, hot and moist with the breeze unable to spill down over the lip. I traverse the steep incline which is a mixture of occasional stairs and a hacked-out pathway. Twists and turns break down the slope in places while ladder-like ascents conquer the climb in others.

As I sight the peak ahead, a shadowy grey form passes almost silently overhead. Its massive silhouette is the unmistakable shape of the venerable B-52, its wings swept back, and it is soon gone, as mystically as it came. I pause on a landing, mid-ascent, where a rusting winch looks out to sea. At my altitude, a C-130 Hercules cranks about an invisible pole in a steep turn over a speck in the ocean. My eyes adjust beyond the glare of the waves and I sight a vessel beneath the Hercules' curious gaze. Then it levels its wings and sets course away from me towards the horizon.

At the peak I climb inside a bunker from World War Two and survey the coast beneath me. Its walls are thick and the air inside is dark, still and cool. The colourful helicopters and bright sails of the boats below seem to be at odds with the sombre atmosphere of the bunker. Up here the breeze has returned and swirls past me as I regroup and begin the more speedy descent.

Whether I am retracing my path through the crater to the drum of a Blackhawk hovering above or lowering my cutlery momentarily in the evening to catch a glimpse of the Boeing eerily entering the cloud above, the skies always seem to be filled. And no matter how sincerely I might have intended to go cold turkey, the truth is that my eyes will always be cast skyward at the hint of an aircraft above.

As surely as I checked my footing with each step as I climbed the crater, I will check the sky for signs of life. Be it the graceful lines of a soaring hawk or the brute force of a B-52, the act of flight cannot help but captivate me.

As the Boeing raised its nose to take me home, thin whisps of vapour danced back over the wing, growing stronger as we banked smoothly in the tropical air. With the wingtip climbing into the sky, my window filled with clear blue sky. A blue that is only interrupted by the outline of a dark grey dart as a Raptor rockets into the stratosphere. I guess when flight is in your blood, there really is no escape.

***

45

Captured in Time

The walls are covered in charts and the orders of the day. A wireless continually relays the latest updates, only occasionally interrupted by a new message clattering over the teletype. Across the large oak desk from me sits a Coast Guard Commander, punching down on the keys of his typewriter with intent, only pausing to question me about today's sortie. The look on his brow is no-nonsense, for today is December 10th, 1941 and I am about to overfly the devastated Pearl Harbor...

Of course, the year is actually 2014, but Bruce Mayes of Pacific Warbirds has created a setting so real that it is hard not to be caught up in the moment. A former Army and Coast Guard pilot, Bruce has flown everything from Hueys to Hercules, but equally fascinating is that Bruce is a native of Oahu and grew up surrounded by the airfields and artefacts of the attack on Pearl Harbor. Combined with his accumulated knowledge on the subject, his insight is both detailed and personal.

The icing on the cake is that today we will fly over Bruce's historic homeland in a World War Two vintage T-6 SNJ trainer, painted in the markings of a "tail hook" from the USS Saratoga. First, we must brief the mission, a simulated photographic reconnaissance flight that will circumnavigate the island via a list of significant waypoints from that fateful day. As I take up my seat in the adjoining briefing room, Bruce discusses the facts just as they were known three days after the attack. He speaks of the two waves of Japanese aircraft that struck that Sunday morning and reviews copies of original orders and signals.

I am shown photographic images and short films, estimated casualties and damage to the fleet. All the while I am steadily appreciating the scope of the attack beyond the shores of Pearl Harbor. The airfields, the radar station, the diverted bombers and the few allied fighters that were able to bravely offer resistance in the face of overwhelming numbers. The raw footage and cold statistics are sobering and strike with a deeper impact than any Hollywood blockbuster could ever hope to achieve. Now it is time to fly.

Parachute on and strapped in low and tight, I rehearse the bailout drill for my position in the rear seat. Headset off, unstrap harness, lock canopy open and dive over the right-hand side of the cockpit, aiming for the wing's trailing edge. As I repeat the drill, I survey that everything about this aircraft exudes an air of safe passage and security, from the girder-like framework that envelopes me, to the sizeable North American rudder pedals in front. Bruce's voice breaks through my earpieces as he completes his checklists and brings the aeroplane to life with a puff of exhaust smoke and a throaty roar of the Pratt and Whitney radial engine. The two propeller blades have now blurred into a lone spinning disc and the instruments ahead of me have come to life.

We weave our way to the runway in true tail-wheel style and my mind drifts to the mass of young aviators whose rudder pedals danced this dance in a very different time. Lined up on the centreline, the throttle is smoothly opened, and I sink reassuringly into my seat. Soon the tail rises and then the aircraft's shadow falls away, skipping past the last remaining wartime hangar of Barber's Field. We are underway.

We roll gently to the left and set course to the north with the famous harbor out to our right. All the while Bruce details the significance of the sights as they pass below. Wheeler Field where the P-40 Warhawks had been ablaze now hosts a fleet of Blackhawk helicopters on the very same tarmac. The lesser-known coral runway, from where two young Army Air Corps pilots took off into a hostile sky, has now been all but reclaimed by vegetation. The site of the radar station that first detected the inbound Japanese armada of the skies and was mistaken for B-17 Flying Fortresses inbound from the mainland. Bellows Airfield and the beach where a midget submarine had been dragged onshore. The points of interest are numerous.

One by one the historic waypoints slide beneath the canary yellow wings of the SNJ, set to a backdrop of pristine waters, lush green valleys and jutting igneous ridge lines born of a volcanic past. Such a setting seems to be so at odds with the devastation that took place that December morning over 70 years ago.

Still, as I sit beneath the greenhouse-style canopy with the barest of instrumentation in front of me there is a sense of that time. As I wheel to the left and right I am struck by the reality that these were the same parcels of space through which the Japanese fighters and bombers had passed en route to their targets.

We slip between two jagged peaks to emerge with Waikiki in the distance on our left and Pearl Harbor straight ahead. Ford Island, with its runway and orange-and-white-striped control tower looms large, as does the massive battleship Missouri, now at anchor and standing watch over the sunken USS Arizona. The Arizona with its more than 1,000 souls still at rest beneath the waves is one of the most moving places I have ever visited.

My heart aches for those lost lives and yet my mind cannot help but imagine how crowded the skies must have been on that December day. For the sky over Pearl Harbour is relatively small in area, yet it must have been brimming with the swirling mass of attacking aircraft. Months in planning, the co-ordinated Japanese airborne assault must have created chaos on the ground. Caught off-guard and scrambling to fathom what was taking place, the defenders did their best to return fire but the skies still wreaked havoc on the earth below.

From my vantage point overhead, I can picture the white wake of the torpedoes threading towards "battleship row". Like the Arizona, the USS Utah still sits "on the bottom" and I can visualise the USS Nevada making its failed dash for the open seas, ultimately being crippled and beached in order to keep the lifeline entrance to the harbor unobstructed. The smell of burning oil and the rising funnels of black smoke. The noise must have been deafening on land, sea and in the air.

In contrast, the skies today are clear and blue, and the only sound is the rhythmic, reliable hum of the SNJ's engine. There is hardly a ripple in the air or on the water and the magic of flight is at its very best. The here-and-now is in stark contrast with history, as the outline of the sunken Arizona can still be seen through the crystal-clear waters as I pass overhead. This single image breaks through my wistful pondering of flight and prevents me from being solely lost in the moment. Nor should I, as this is a site of solemn significance and deserves respect and remembrance.

The USS Missouri and Ford Island slip from view behind the tailplane and our nose is once again pointed towards Barber's Field. The runways, hangars and shoreline loom ahead as green fields and a rust-coloured quarry pass below. Bruce's words leave the past and return to the present as checklists are recited and power settings adjusted. The SNJ is readied for its return to earth and manoeuvred past the huge white tanks of the refinery and the clean white sands of the beaches.

I look down at the water and waves off the wing tip as the nose rolls about the horizon to align with the runway. With gear and flaps extended, the airfield fence passes by and we arrive over the threshold. The wheels touch down and eventually the blurred disc again becomes two stationary propeller blades. I slide the canopy back, with my harness and headset still in place, and a hint of oil fumes mingles with the salt air. Leaning my head back all I can see is the blue sky, bordered by the framework of the 1940s cockpit. There are no visual cues of the present as I look into those historic skies above me. That very same piece of sky, but in such a very different time.

***

Captured in Time. The SNJ and its shadow become airborne on Oahu.

My daughter reflects on her grandfather's cockpit.

46

A Matter of Trust

As a young pilot I shared the same frustrations as just about every other young pilot waiting to move up to the next level. Whether it was that first job on a multi-engined aeroplane or cracking that elusive airline job, there always seemed to be something a little greener sitting just over the fence.

I was knocking on doors and writing letters to companies until my knuckles were raw and my hands ached, but it was all to no avail. Charter companies were not hiring, and if they were, I didn't have the hours in my log book to ever be considered. It seemed that to fly a six-seat Beechcraft Baron you needed a PhD and six million hours flying the space shuttle. I was continually reminded that these were "high-performance machines" and experienced pilots were lining up to fly them.

My only chance was to leave the city and head west to the outback. There were country towns where aviation was a lifeline and if you were prepared to live in the middle of nowhere, then there just may be an opportunity. These towns were also full of young "pilots in waiting", but at least they were of a similar experience level to me. In fact, the joke used to be that if you wanted a pilot, just shake a tree and they would fall out. In reality, they were in abundance, but they were working in bars, picking fruit and driving taxis; anything to earn an income until that flying job came along.

I was fortunate and, subject to the mandatory check-ride, I secured a job as soon as I arrived in town – Kununurra in far-northern Western Australia. I was to start by flying single-engined Cessnas, but with the potential to move up to twin-engined Cessnas and Pipers. I couldn't wait and, after the chief pilot checked me out in a company aircraft, an amazing thing happened: They sent me to work.

That might not sound that strange, but at the city airfield I had left, there were a number of hoops to jump through before you were actually allowed to fly. All of a sudden, here I was: my name was written on the roster board and aircraft registrations and destinations were being penned-in beside my name. I stood there open-mouthed, which caught the attention of the boss and drew him away from filling in the rest of the board. I explained that this was a little quicker advancement than where I'd come from, to which he replied – with a good deal of mirth –.

So started one of the most enjoyable chapters of my entire aviation career. The next day I flew with a senior pilot beside me over the scenic tourist route which was the company's bread and butter; the day after that I flew it alone. A week later I was despatched on a charter flight to a remote township with just a map and the aircraft's compass, but once again under the watchful eye of a senior pilot. The next flight into the outback I flew solo.

I was amazed at the level of trust they placed in me and my fellow pilots. We were young and relatively inexperienced, but they respected that we held a commercial pilot's licence and that was good enough for them. After a few flights with senior pilots, we were let loose to fly across the border and into the desert without restriction. Sometimes the flights were with geologists, not to "real" runways, but rather landing strips scratched out of clearings in the Spinifex at a stated latitude and longitude. There wasn't a GPS on board, so you navigated by flying your heading, watching the clock and paying attention to the distinctive shapes and colours of the clay pans along the way. By the end of the day, the chart would be covered with times and notations pencilled across the landscape.

Then there were days when the weather was low and an aboriginal tribal elder at an outback community wished to be ferried across to another settlement. He would point out the bend in the creek bed on my map and I would calculate a heading and a time interval, just as I had been trained. As we launched off across the Never Never, I would studiously guide my aircraft towards the destination until a weathered hand would reach forward and point in a slightly different direction. Sure enough, there would be a small strip amongst the scrub right where the finger was pointing. For all of my training, these natives of the land were expert navigators at sea level or in the air.

As the years passed, I flew increasingly larger aircraft, with a flight-deck door separating me from the passengers. Then, after 9/11, the flight-deck door was bolted shut and pilots became even further removed from the folks who filled the seats. Conversely, the people who would steer them safely to their destination became virtual spectres, only seen momentarily here and there. Still, passengers have maintained their trust in the "faceless few" and air travel has fought back from those shocking terror attacks in New York.

At so many levels, aviation is founded on trust. Whether it is a flight instructor allowing the student to land for that very first time, or a pilot's acceptance that an aircraft is signed out and serviceable, there is something more than a procedure involved. There is one human being respecting another enough to entrust lives into their care. It is also more than recognising the qualifications of another professional, as there are numerous fields where the diplomas on the wall couldn't convince the majority to put their lives in another's hands.

Like airmanship itself, there is a deeper bond that is difficult to put into words. Whether it is between engineer and pilot, pilots and passengers or among the crew of an aircraft, there is something more. It is a mutual respect in the other's role that exceeds any supporting documentation or certification. It is wonderful human quality. It is a matter of trust.

***

47

Fly By Night

There is something very different about flying at night; something beyond the darkness. It reveals sights that are unseen by day and yet conceals threats that are obvious in the sun's bright rays. It is another world with another set of challenges for those who fly.

A clear starry night in smooth air is something to behold. Removed from the glare of city lights and above the pollution and particles that fill the air, the sky is a sea of pin-pricks of light. The reflection of satellites in low orbit is easy to spot and the flashes of light from "space junk" burning up on re-entry are eye-catching. The dim glow of the instruments add to the peaceful mood until the next squawking radio transmission interrupts the peace.

For the student pilot there is an initial excitement that drowns out any contemplation of the potential dangers of flight by night. The airport has transformed into a trail of bright coloured lights that lead to the runway's end. And the take-off now becomes a transition from visual flight to a reliance on the instruments as the runway falls away and the horizon disappears. The information from those instruments is critical as the body can interpret acceleration as a climb and constant turns as level flight. The argument between the senses has brought many night pilots to grief.

The parallel lights of the runway can restore some logic and become a critical term of reference all the way around the pattern until the wheels once again touch the earth. All the while, the pilot balances the information being provided by visual cues and the flight instruments. It is a brave new world that takes on another face when navigation exercises take the trainee beyond the bounds of the airfield and across the countryside.

When the moon is bright, the earth below can be seen quite clearly and these are the nights that single-engined aircraft should fly if the need is imperative. On these nights, individual sheep can be seen grazing and there is a slight possibility of successfully landing in a paddock should the engine fail. In contrast, dark nights conceal the terrain and can send a shudder of contemplation up the spine. For in the darkness below await the jaws of inhospitable trees and ravines, ready to swallow those whose luck has run out.

Similarly, the night sky ahead can conceal towering clouds and turbulence. Weather radar can provide an early warning to those who are appropriately equipped, but for the less fortunate it is a case of squinting into the blackness with nothing to focus upon. Sometimes the absence of stars ahead can suggest that something more sinister lurks on the horizon.

Gaining an awareness of these variables is when the student pilot often begins to appreciate the potentially grave consequences of flying by night. Partly instilled by staring at the abyss below and inevitably reinforced by the instructor shuffling uncomfortably in the other seat. The normally smooth hum of the engine doubles in importance and every slight arrhythmia in its tone causes the pilot's heart to miss a beat.

Still, if the apprehension can be put to one side, there is no arguing the beauty beyond the windshield. Highways become twisted ribbons of light, with townships bulging and branching off the main route. City skylines combine brilliant white towers with spots of scarlet and blue beaming from billboards. Stadiums are bright green islands while boats are little more than specks of light scampering along the black waterways. The familiar tapestry below is transformed into a light show once the sun has set.

For some, they will rarely fly at night once the qualification has been earned. And then there are those who will ply their trade by moonlight. Freight pilots, medivac crew and long-haul airline pilots to list just a few.

The night can be a lonely place for the single pilot with only a load of freight as a companion and the occasional blinking lights of another aircraft passing by. On the ground at some remote airfield, a hurried conversation and a hot drink from a flask provide a break in proceedings and then it is time to get underway again. Medivac pilots may view the night through the green of their night vision goggles, or make an approach to land on a runway illuminated by car headlights or flares. For these pilots no two nights are ever the same and their destination is a mystery when they sign on for duty.

On an international carrier's flight deck, the mood is often mellow with only stilted conversation. With the autopilot engaged the crew are often fighting off the urge to sleep by drinking another coffee or reviewing the latest weather forecasts for the 50th time. The remaining miles counting down on the flight management computer can be daunting and a degree of relief is found when it finally ticks below one thousand. Until that time, the miles, borders and time-zones slip silently beneath the fuselage while hundreds of passengers sleep soundly in the cabin.

Whether the aircraft has one engine and four seats or four engines and a small population on board, the night sky contains both mystery and magic. The spectacular Northern Lights are invisible by day, but by night their dancing green blanket is world renowned. The eruption of lightning within a cloud can illuminate the darkest sky and the Milky Way sits overhead to remind us just how insignificant we really are. The night provides a second sky over this third rock from the sun.

Once again, as pilots, we are privileged to enter this nocturnal realm. To look up and see the magnificent array of stars, or to cast our eyes downward and look upon the earth in a very different way to those that are land-locked in slumber. For all of its hidden threats, there are far more benefits. The clear star-filled sky is a truly beautiful place and we possess a front row seat to view this magnificent show when we leave the earth and fly by night.

***

48

Too Often Forgotten

The news was fresh on the Internet and the smoke was still hanging ominously in the air. A fire-bombing aircraft fighting a bush inferno had crashed and its pilot had perished. Heroic helicopters attempting to reach the site had been repelled by the smoke and hot gusty winds, and all the while the fire raged on. Once again, life had been lost in the service of others. Once again and not for the last time.

I recalled a Christmas Eve a few years past when a paramedic died attempting to rescue another as he was winched below the beating blades of a helicopter towards the rugged rock face. And a Medivac flight some years ago that crashed and killed all on board. They are now headlines that have long faded, but the memories are still clear. Each one a tragedy that left families and friends forever changed.

It is an aspect of aviation that operates almost by stealth. Aside from the occasional news bulletin showing a stranded sailor being winched on board a helicopter as it hovers above the waves, little is there to be seen. And the heroes remain anonymous. Like an iceberg, the greatest mass of their effort floats silently beneath the surface. All the while we sleep a little more soundly knowing that they are there should we need them.

And on those dark nights when we are loathe to venture out, they are landing on highways illuminated by car lights or descending into some obscure clearing that glows green through the night-vision goggles. Often their operations take place at the limits of man and machine in a realm where most never venture. We sit safely, secure in our buffer zones with clear skies and fair winds.

Theirs is not bravado, but accepted risk after hours upon hours of training and rehearsing. Years of experience that can be channelled into moments of intense concentration and selfless effort. And still, sometimes it can still go wrong and loss of life results. When this happens, their comrades must still maintain their focus and respond should the alarm sound in the very next minute.

These emergency services are part of the broader aviation community; an industry that, is too often maligned. The noisy airports are always too close and nobody wants a flightpath within a thousand miles of their backyard. They see aircraft as dangerous vehicles waiting to fall from the sky and carelessly pumping out pollutants in the meantime. Everyone wants the security and safety on offer, but no-one wants it next door. And that thumping overhead, the one that stirred them from their sleep was more than a mere disturbance, more than a nuisance. It was the rotors carefully lifting a young child from one hospital bed to another where a team of surgeons was waiting.

Aviation wears many clothes. Those which the general public perceive are the necessary evil of airliners and the light aircraft that make up the sport of kings. If the truth be known, those airliners contribute to the nation's economy in so many ways, while most aircraft owners and private pilots are scratching to find the funds to pursue their passion. However, in the public arena perception can become reality and the good is washed away by the media-conjured controversy.

Immune to the barbs, the heroes in our midst keep going about their work; training and preparing, always at the ready when the phone rings. And when it does ring, they are on the move in minutes. Flight plans are compiled in minutes and briefings pieced together as the few known facts are relayed. En route, the picture may evolve a little further, but often the flights are made into the relative unknown.

Only when they arrive can a full appreciation of the task at hand be grasped and a plan of attack formulated. Whether it calls for the extrication of an injured person or the tactical drop of retardant on an uncontrollable fire front, the crew must adapt to the situation confronting them. And when the training template doesn't quite fit, they must adapt, improvise and overcome, all the while keeping the safety of their crew and their craft paramount.

Should the cards fall cruelly as they did this week, and another life is lost, we should all pause and truly consider what has occurred. A father, a son, a sister or wife has left this world in the process of protecting another. Be it property or life at stake, this person has given up their tomorrows to help total strangers in their time of need. Their intent had always been to return home safely, but always in that suppressed corner of the mind they also knew there was a chance they might just not make it one day...but not today.

Military and civilian, professional and volunteer, men and women. They are a special breed that places the welfare of others so highly. Their availability is around the clock and without question; their family lives are ruled by rosters. They have missed more birthdays and been late for more dinners than they care to remember. Yet, tomorrow they will once again don their flying suits with reflective stripes and secure the helmets that complete their anonymity.

Bright crests on their shoulders and the flanks of their machines denote their cause, but only a small embroidered patch on the chest identifies the individual. For most, that is how they wish it to be, for they are part of a team and it is only as a functioning team that they can surmount the deadly challenges they face. A small nametag is fine by them; those who matter already know their name.

Their anonymity should not exclude them from our admiration and support. We should recognise what it is they do every day, far away from the headlines. They are true heroes and, like so many real heroes, they are too often forgotten.

***

49

CONTRAILS IN COMMON

I sat on the back step of my home and surveyed the newly mown lawn and contemplated the edges of grass that still needed to be clipped. As I am prone to do, my eyes drifted skyward where a Boeing was plying the stock route from Sydney to Melbourne with a distinct white contrail in its wake. Incongruous to the sight of a high-level jet came the familiar drone of a small piston engine from beyond the tree line.

Soon a small training aircraft emerged, a Piper, and definitely without a contrail behind. Yet, from where I sat, its flight path was virtually identical to that of the jet 30,000 feet above it and it appeared to be tethered to the higher aircraft. Louder and louder the drone became until the Piper passed overhead low enough for me to read the registration on its wings, but not to see the face of the pilot within. However, if I had been able to see who was at the helm, what would have been the scene?

On such a beautiful day was it a private pilot out for a local jaunt with a friend? Perhaps a businessman on his way to the nation's capital for a lunchtime meeting? Or was it a young student pilot, diligently navigating as their finger traced the pencil line on their chart, despite the challenge of training, revelling in their new-found freedom.

I had a fair idea of the scene in the contrail-pulling jet above. They would be mid-route, comfortably in the cruise phase of flight and anticipating their arrival instructions into Melbourne. More than likely, one of the pilots would be consuming their breakfast before briefings and flight duties consumed their attention. Despite their experience and the sense of routine, they would still be taking in the sight of the crisp, clear sky outside their window.

They will be in Melbourne in half an hour having hurtled through the sky at eight miles each minute. There may be some weather loitering above their destination, but their equipment and training will make negotiating that cloud layer rather straightforward. Even so, they'll brief the expectation of an approach on instruments, just to be safe.

Far below, the Piper continued on its way at a leisurely two miles each minute. However, there is no autopilot and no flight management computer. At best, I'd suspect there may be a small GPS unit, but regardless, the pilot is having to hand-fly their aircraft as they attend to all of the other duties. The occasional bump of rising air or distraction attempts to unseat the tiny aeroplane from level flight, but its vigilant pilot is there to right the ship and double-check just where they are.

The pilot catches sight of the contrail far above and stretching into the distance ahead. A small white-winged dot sits millimetres ahead of the steam of water vapour it is generating in the upper atmosphere. The youngster marvels at the scene above; its speed, its distance from the earth. "One day, yes one day, I'll be there", daydreaming for just a moment before turning on the auxiliary pump and readying to change fuel tanks.

The air up there just looks more pure to the beginner down "amongst the weeds". That tiny dart ahead of the contrail looks so sleek that it is not merely flying quickly but appears to be tearing through the very fabric of the sky. And the equipment on that flight deck must be amazing, but the view, oh the view. Up there those guys must look down on the world as if they own it. Unlimited visibility and the training and tools to proceed even when the sky isn't clear.

They aren't flying with one eye watching the ground rise and the cloud grow lower. They aren't paying an hourly hire rate and sweating on the total of the invoice. Their cabin heater works, and the labels haven't rubbed off half of their switches. They aren't struggling to reach the half-stale sandwich in the backpack that has slipped...just...out...of...reach. "One day, yes one day, I'll be there."

The railway line is now crossing the road and the high-voltage power lines are sitting out to the right-hand side. Check the time, set the new heading and start turning towards the two lakes. The Piper feels as if it is part of the scenery, flying so low in comparison to the jet towering overhead. Meanwhile at 37,000 feet the flight crew look out the window with their eyes cast down at the landscape below.

At such a height, towns become patches rather than individual buildings. Major highways join those same towns, but any smaller roads are nearly invisible. The captain lowers his sunglasses and squints, trying to make out a seaside village where he holidayed a few years ago. He thinks he sights it but can't really be sure. Out the other window the first officer spots a couple of lakes and thinks back to his days of flight training and checking his position over those same lakes as a fledgling aviator. Those were the days.

Map in hand, everything was so close by. The earth had features, genuine landmarks. You could see individual homes and even see if there were people swimming in their pool. Flying from turning point to turning point until another dusty little airport appeared in the windscreen. Then came the challenge of making the right calls and joining the circuit just as the rules dictate, landing on a tiny grass runway because the crosswind was too great for the little machine to land on the asphalt. That was flying.

The sun glints off the lakes far below, but there is another speck of reflection. A speck of white, flickering in the sun. A few minutes pass and it glints again, having moved a tiny distance towards the lakes. "Perhaps it's a light aircraft down amongst the weeds", the first officer thinks with a tinge of envy. Part of him longs for those days and it crosses his mind to perhaps hire a small aircraft, do some training and step back in time. Now that would be a change from the norm.

Real flying. He pauses a moment, excited at the thought, "One day, yes one day, I'll be there."

***

50

MY LIFE OF FLIGHT

Eighteen-thousand hours, 30 years, 70 different types of aeroplanes, and more destinations than I can count. Miles, minutes or moments, do we ever really measure a lifetime of flight? I'm sure that it can be boxed and parcelled up from a broad range of perspectives, but somehow it loses something when we do that. We inevitably quantify portions at the expense of the broader, wonderful experience. For me my life in the air has been about something more.

One night I sat in a Boeing 747 over the middle of the Pacific Ocean with pitch-black skies above and waters beneath. The only light was the glow of the instrument panels on our faces as we watched the miles to Los Angeles count down. The captain was a kindly soul who was approaching retirement, while I was a junior Second Officer and a refugee from a recently collapsed airline. With good intent, the captain reflected on his wonderful career and sympathised with the rotten hand I had been dealt when the administrators stepped in and I became a pilot without an airline.

I appreciated the sentiment, but in reality, I saw it very differently. The airline's collapse had disadvantaged me in terms of my career as well as in so many other ways. Ultimately, however, it proved to be an outcome not without benefits. I had been thrown out of my comfort zone and awakened from the treadmill of a job for life. Now I had seen the world from the flight deck, pursued further studies for a degree of security and chased passions lost somewhere along the way. Yet again, to pivot my life in aviation about that one event is to focus on one negative in a line of positive twists of fate.

I was fortunate from the outset to have been born into an aviation family with a father who mentored me from the time I could walk. For as long as my memory stretches, I was sitting beside him in a cockpit somewhere, hanging on his every word. I was never pushed towards this vocation but encouraged whenever my interest in flight was there to be seen. I would sit for hours on my rooftop with binoculars and watch the passing parade in the sky, impatient for my turn.

I was blessed to have the opportunities afforded me as a teenager in the Air Force cadets, including a scholarship for those first few hours of training. And when the training became full-blooded, I was blessed that my father took the reins and poured hours into my education in the classroom and in the air. I am thankful for the years spent as a paramedic to appreciate how great the gift of life is and to never forget the privilege to be crossing the skies when real heroes are on the streets below me helping strangers.

That my career has brought some close calls has taught me some of the most valuable lessons. I have buried far too many friends for whom the lurking demons of flight struck with an unforgiving finality. Then there are those friends who have made the journey with me and whose sons and daughters now cast model gliders into the sky with my children. My gorgeous wife is a pilot, brought to me through flight, with a shared passion that saw us looking in the same direction as often as we looked into each other's eyes.

I have lived to see a world that once only lived in books and atlases spread across my bedroom floor. There have been peoples, cultures and places that have taken my breath away and sights that live vividly in my mind's eye. I have watched wild camels race across the desert floor into canyons with palm trees that time had forgotten and seen the brilliant tail of a rocket as it began its journey into space. The horizon has at times been too distant to focus on and it has tumbled at such a rate that the only option was to let it become a blur. There has been lightning launching vertically up into the clear night sky and days so hot that I thirstily sheltered beneath the belly of my tiny aeroplane awaiting my passengers' return.

I could not agree with the kind captain's sentiments. I have been blessed to travel those invisible roads in the sky and I give thanks each time the wheels leave the earth, and again when they safely touch down at the end of the day. It is a privilege to fly and see the sky not as the limit, but as a second home.

So, is there really any point at the end of a career to look back and really measure a life of flight? I don't think so, but I'll let you know when I get there.

***

Too Often Forgotten. The NSW Ambulance helicopter readies for departure.

My Life of Flight.

ACKNOWLEDGEMENTS

First and foremost, I would like to thank my wonderful wife and tremendous children for their patience and support as I have ventured far and wide, only to return home and type away on the keyboard.

Thanks to my numerous magazine editors who have published my work over the years and continue to introduce me to new and exciting opportunities in the aviation world. A special thanks to the team at 'Australian Aviation' magazine; who have become more friends than colleagues over the years. Also, thanks to all of the generous contributors of images for this book including Anthony Jackson, Tim Visser, Stephen Brown and Paul Sadler.

Thank you to all of my friends and fellow aviators for playing such a special role in this journey. And to my cherished mates who have left this life in pursuit of your passion; you will never be forgotten. To the air crew who have shared the flight deck and the aviation enthusiasts who have shared their passion. Thank you.

Finally, a sincere thank you to you…the readers of this book. Your continued warm response to my books inspires me to continue writing and share my tales from the sky.

***

www.ingramcontent.com/pod-product-compliance
Lightning Source LLC
Chambersburg PA
CBHW071900290426
44110CB00013B/1222